Managing State in Flutter Pragmatically

Discover how to adopt the best state management approach for scaling your Flutter app

Waleed Arshad

Packt‹t›

BIRMINGHAM—MUMBAI

Managing State in Flutter Pragmatically

Copyright © 2021 Packt Publishing

Assistant Group Product Manager: Pavan Ramchandani
Publishing Product Manager: Kaustubh Manglurkar
Senior Editor: Keagan Carneiro
Content Development Editor: Adrija Mitra
Technical Editor: Shubham Sharma
Copy Editor: Safis Editing
Project Coordinator: Rashika Ba
Proofreader: Safis Editing
Indexer: Manju Arasan
Production Designer: Sinhayna Bais

First published: November, 2021

Production reference: 1291021

Published by Packt Publishing Ltd.
Livery Place
35 Livery Street
Birmingham
B3 2PB, UK.

ISBN 978-1-80107-077-5

www.packt.com

To my parents, Raheela Perveen and M. Arshad, and to my wife, Safa.

– Waleed Arshad

Contributors

About the author

Waleed Arshad is a core mobile technologist and a passionate cross-platform developer. He is the first person from Pakistan to become a Google Developer Expert in Flutter. Since graduating from FAST-NUCES Karachi, he has been working in the industry for more than 5 years and is currently working in the Developer Experience team for Flutter at Tendermint Inc. He also holds a master's in computer science from the Institute of Business Administration, Karachi. As a community leader at Flutter Karachi, Pakistan, he has organized substantial physical and online events in Karachi, along with having the honor of speaking at different events and venues across the globe.

About the reviewer

Nishant Srivastava is an Android engineer with experience developing mobile apps/SDKs for the Android platform. He is passionate about working at the intersection of hardware and software, focusing on firmware and audio engineering. He is an open source enthusiast and contributes to the ecosystem in various formats, such as conference talks, blog posts, books, and podcasts.

In the past, he has coauthored *Kotlin Coroutines by Tutorial (Raywenderlich Team)* and tech-reviewed *Seven Mobile Apps in Seven Weeks: Native Apps, Multiple Platforms (Pragmatic Programmer)*, *Beginning Android Game Development (4th Ed., Apress)*, and *Learning Java by Building Android Games (3rd Ed., Packt)*.

Table of Contents

Section 2: Types, Techniques, and Approaches

3
Diving into Advanced State Management Approaches

4
Adopting State Management Approaches from React

5

Executing Distinctive Approaches Like GetX, GetIt, and Binder

Section 3: Code-Level Implementation

6

Creating a Shopping Cart Application Using Basic Approaches

Other Books You May Enjoy

Index

Preface

This book is a definitive guide for people who are starting out with Flutter and want to learn about state management, and also those who have some sort of background in state management but they either use one solution for everything or get confused with what technique to use. The book will take a hands-on approach wherein we will first cover the basics related to state management in Flutter and quickly dive into building and manipulating a shopping cart app using all the popular approaches, such as BloC/Cubit, Provider, MobX, Riverpod, and so on, for managing state in Flutter. We will also learn how to adopt approaches from React, such as Redux and all its flavors.

Flutter is a cross-platform UI toolkit that enables developers to create beautiful native applications for mobile, desktop, and the web with a single code base. State management is one of the most crucial and complex topics within Flutter, having a decent learning curve that users have struggled with – mainly due to the wide array of approaches available.

Who this book is for

This book is for developers who have already started their Flutter journey and are now looking to learn about optimal state management approaches for their app development journey. The book will also help junior Flutter engineers to find the best state management solution that fits their app. This will also help Flutter engineers to learn which state management should be used under what circumstances.

What this book covers

Chapter 1, *States and State Management Overview*, covers all the basic understanding of state in Flutter, how it affects our application, how it affects our approach to writing code, and how changes in state affect the application in general.

Chapter 2, The Core Building Blocks of State Management, takes a deep dive into the implementations of the core building blocks of state management approaches, starting from `setState()`, which is the first approach and the default implemented technique when a new Flutter application is created, followed by `InheritedWidget` and `InheritedModel`, which are helpful when the scope of the application is expanded.

Chapter 3, Diving into Advanced State Management Approaches, describes in detail the intermediate-advanced level of approaches used in the larger part of the Flutter application development world, starting with BLoC and Cubit, driving down to Provider and its refactored implementation, Riverpod.

Chapter 4, Adopting State Management Approaches from React, takes a look at the approaches in Flutter that are from React. This includes the famous Redux approach and its flavors, Fish-Redux and MobX.

Chapter 5, Executing Distinctive Approaches like GetX, GetIt, and Binder, discusses the approaches that most people use for their convenience and code style. We will discuss the theory and concepts behind GetX, GetIt, and Binder.

Chapter 6, Creating a Shopping Cart Application Using Basic Approaches, describes how to code a shopping cart application using basic approaches.

Chapter 7, Manipulating a Shopping Cart Application through BLoC, Provider, and React-Based Approaches, takes a deep dive into Provider and React-based approaches. This chapter describes how to code the shopping cart app using some famous approaches.

Chapter 8, Using GetX, GetIt, and Binder to Update the Cart Application, describes how to code shopping cart example applications using some specific, simplified approaches.

Chapter 9, Comparative State Management Analysis: When to Use What?, gives you a clear insight into when to use what. This chapter briefly describes all the techniques discussed in the previous chapters and presents a comparative analysis to help you decide what technique should be used in what sort of situation.

To get the most out of this book

You will need Flutter installed on your system. Complete installation steps can be found at `https://flutter.dev/docs/get-started/install`.

Software/hardware covered in the book	Operating system requirements
Flutter	Windows, macOS, or Linux

You will also need Android Studio installed on your computer in order to test and run for Android. If you are using a Mac and you wish to build for iOS, you will have to install Xcode as well. You can use Android Studio as your IDE for Flutter development, but it is suggested you use VSCode or IntelliJ IDEA as they are recommended IDEs by the Flutter community.

Running and testing will require a real device or a simulator installed on your computer. If you don't want to test Flutter apps on your mobile device, it will be mandatory to install a simulator on your system. For Android, you can simply download and install the simulator through Android Studio (this is for all types of platforms, that is, macOS, Windows, Linux). For building on iOS, you will automatically get a simulator application when you install Xcode on your Mac.

If you are using the digital version of this book, we advise you to type the code yourself or access the code from the book's GitHub repository (a link is available in the next section). Doing so will help you avoid any potential errors related to the copying and pasting of code.

Download the example code files

You can download the example code files for this book from GitHub at `https://github.com/PacktPublishing/Managing-State-in-Flutter-Pragmatically`. If there's an update to the code, it will be updated in the GitHub repository.

We also have other code bundles from our rich catalog of books and videos available at `https://github.com/PacktPublishing/`. Check them out!

Download the color images

We also provide a PDF file that has color images of the screenshots and diagrams used in this book. You can download it here: `https://static.packt-cdn.com/downloads/9781801070775_ColorImages.pdf`

Conventions used

There are a number of text conventions used throughout this book.

`Code in text`: Indicates code words in the text, database table names, folder names, filenames, file extensions, pathnames, dummy URLs, user input, and Twitter handles. Here is an example: "As soon as the page loads, it will check whether our `CartModel` instance is ready."

A block of code is set as follows:

```
class CartModel {
  List<Item> cart;

  CartModel({required this.cart});
}
```

When we wish to draw your attention to a particular part of a code block, the relevant lines or items are set in bold:

```
@override
Widget build(BuildContext context) {
  // One
  var model = getIt<CartModel>();
  var cart = model.cart;
```

Any command-line input or output is written as follows:

```
flutter packages pub run build_runner build
```

Bold: Indicates a new term, an important word, or words that you see onscreen. For instance, words in menus or dialog boxes appear in **bold**. Here is an example: "Type each one of the libraries mentioned previously and pick their latest dependency from their websites' **Installing** tabs."

> **Tips or important notes**
> Appear like this.

Get in touch

Feedback from our readers is always welcome.

General feedback: If you have questions about any aspect of this book, email us at customercare@packtpub.com and mention the book title in the subject of your message.

Errata: Although we have taken every care to ensure the accuracy of our content, mistakes do happen. If you have found a mistake in this book, we would be grateful if you would report this to us. Please visit www.packtpub.com/support/errata and fill in the form.

Piracy: If you come across any illegal copies of our works in any form on the internet, we would be grateful if you would provide us with the location address or website name. Please contact us at copyright@packt.com with a link to the material.

If you are interested in becoming an author: If there is a topic that you have expertise in and you are interested in either writing or contributing to a book, please visit authors.packtpub.com.

Share Your Thoughts

Once you've read *Managing State in Flutter Pragatically* , we'd love to hear your thoughts! Scan the QR code below to go straight to the Amazon review page for this book and share your feedback.

https://packt.link/r/1-801-07077-6

Your review is important to us and the tech community and will help us make sure we're delivering excellent quality content.

Section 1: The Basics of State Management

In this section, we will explore what a state in Flutter is, what state management is, and why it is so important.

This section comprises the following chapters:

1
States and State Management Overview

This chapter is an introduction to the core concepts of states and state management in Flutter. You will learn the basic important concepts of a state in Flutter and how it affects your application in general. You will also learn about state management, what it is, why it is necessary, and the advantages of using it in your application.

In this chapter, we are going to cover the following main topics:

- What is a state?
- Why is studying states important?
- What is state management?
- Why do we need state management?
- Choosing the best state management technique

This chapter is going to show you why you need to study state management in order to build better, stable, and scalable Flutter applications. By the end of this chapter you will have a grasp of the following:

- The concepts of states and state management in Flutter
- The importance of studying and applying state management in Flutter
- How state and state management are interrelated to each other

Flutter – a brief introduction

Before we jump right into states, state management, and the techniques related to states, we should learn a little about what Flutter is (though this is already this book's pre-requisite).

Flutter is a cross-platform development toolkit that is backed by Google itself. Flutter enables you to create beautiful native applications for iOS, Android, the web, Windows, macOS, Linux, and even embedded systems, *with a single code base.*

Flutter uses Dart, a language created by Google back in October 2011. Dart is easy to learn as it is based on concepts from both open languages such as JavaScript and object-oriented languages such as C# and Java. Dart can be used for client-side programming, such as mobile and web, as well as for server-side development, such as RESTful services.

You can learn more about Flutter and Dart on Flutter's official website (`https://flutter.dev/`).

What is a state?

Before diving into creating applications and managing states in Flutter, it is necessary to understand what a state actually is and how it affects our application.

Put simply, the state of an application is a condition or a situation – an instance or a snapshot that shows the condition of your application at a certain point in time.

For example, your application shows two variables, x and y, with values 2 and 3 respectively. Let's call this state *State A*. Now, if there is a user interaction and the values of your variables x and y change to something else, let's say 4 and 5, that would be a different state of your application, *State B*.

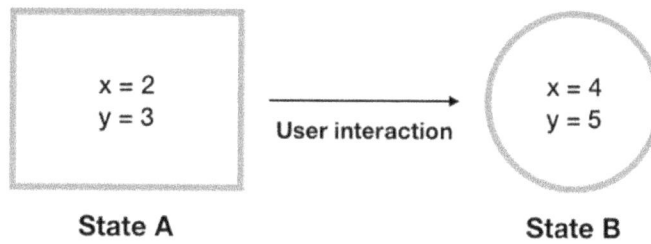

Figure 1.1 – Two different states of an application

States A and B are two different conditions of your application. Each one of them denotes a certain set of values of the variables that can be used to identify which state the application is currently in.

Another example of a state would be a counter application that shows an increasing counter every time the user presses a plus button.

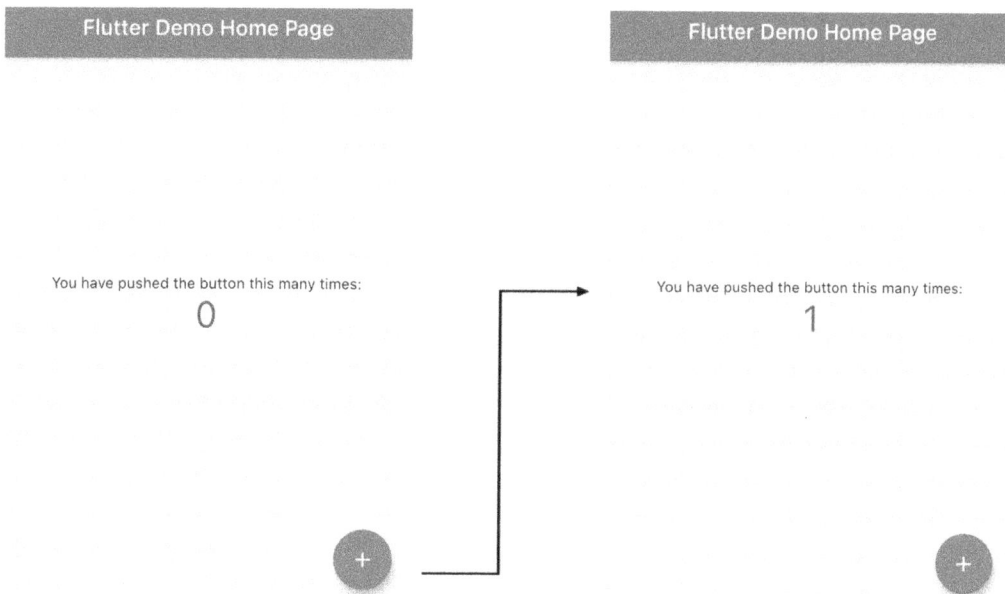

Figure 1.2 – Two different states in a counter example app

The counter keeps on increasing and the state keeps changing as the user presses the plus button.

To summarize, the state shows your application's current set of values and can be changed based on user interaction.

Now we know what a state is, how it is detected and used within an application, and how it affects your application's UI. To better understand states for a large-scale application, let's see why a state is important in an application.

Importance of a state in an application

The state is the core building block of your application. It defines the overall behavior of your app, from the beginning of your user journey to the time the user closes/terminates your application. Every change the user sees is a state of its own, and you need to make sure that your user sees what you intend to show. You also need to make sure that with every possible user interaction, the application shows valid states. It should not show something that you or the user don't expect to see (an exception, a red screen, an unexpected or unhandled error, and so on).

Different states in a large application

Since we now know that every user interaction creates a new state for an application, a complete functional application can have hundreds of states. In order to keep track of and manage every state, it is important to understand what role a state plays inside your application. Here are some examples of states that get updated by user interactions in a simple login page consisting of two text fields and a button:

- The user enters a correct email and password – A new state that navigates the user to some other screen

- The user enters the wrong email and password – A new state showing an error

- The user presses the login button without entering anything – A state that says that the user has to fill in both the required fields

- The user presses the login button with only one filled-in field – A state indicating the field that needs to be filled in

- The internet gets disconnected – A state that shows a pop-up dialog for no internet connection

The preceding example was of one single login page with the three simplest forms of UI components, and you saw how many states were extracted from it. When your application gets bigger, there can be a lot of states to manage. Therefore, studying states and knowing everything about them is as important as building an entire application.

We have seen how important states are and how they help us get the most out of our application. We have also seen the immense importance of states in a larger application with many states. Let's now understand what state management is and how we can manage states in our application through different techniques (the actual point of this book).

What is state management?

State management is simply a technique, or multiple techniques, used to take care of the changes that occur in your application. When your application gets bigger, you need to apply a proper state management approach in order to be able to keep track of every change inside your application and make the application respond to the user accordingly. This can include the following:

- Responding to user interactions

- Keeping track of data throughout the different screens in the application

- Changing data points in the application at one place and handling the response at other points in the app that read that data

This book will show you different techniques of managing states in your Flutter application, ranging from very basic ways, such as `setState` (pushing changes to the UI through a function call), to advanced approaches, such as `BloC` (a business logic component, used to decouple the UI from business logic) and `provider` (a community-favorite technique used widely among a variety of applications).

Choosing the best technique for your application

After finishing this book, you will clearly understand which state management techniques should be used for different kinds of application. It is necessary to be able to figure out the best state management solution for a given kind of application. Remember, there is no one solution that is best for every single application. It is all about choosing the right one for the application you are going to create.

The correct choice of state management solution will enable you to create better, scalable, highly performant, and faster applications with less code mess and better readability.

Using the right approach is going to make your application life cycle easier, as it will enable you to add and update features seamlessly. Also, you will help new developers to understand your code better and adjust with you faster.

Summary

In this chapter, we saw that the state is the condition or situation of your application, giving you a certain set of values for variables inside your application that may or may not be reflected on your screen. When an application transitions from one state to another, the set of values is updated, and a new state is formed and is mostly changed by user interaction.

We studied how many states can be formed with or without user interaction in the case of a simple login screen and the importance of state in a large-scale application. There was an overview of what state management is and why choosing a good state management technique is beneficial to the development life cycle.

In the next chapter, we will discuss the most basic forms of state management techniques, mainly `setState` and `InheritedModel`. We will also see how these approaches are reflected in code with real running examples.

2
The Core Building Blocks of State Management

The next four chapters are about different **state management** techniques, starting from the very basic implementations to diving deep into all sorts of advanced techniques.

In this chapter, we will cover the core building blocks of state management in **Flutter**. We will learn about basic techniques, which include the `setState`, `InheritedWidget`, and `InheritedModel` classes to manage states in Flutter. We will also look at how these approaches are utilized in code with actual implementations.

We will look into the following topics in this chapter:

- `setState()` – Widget-specific state management
- `InheritedWidget` – Top-down approach
- `InheritedModel` – Within the aspect of updating the desired widgets only

This chapter is going to build up your understanding of how basic approaches can be used to detect and track the changes inside a Flutter application. By the end of this chapter, you should be able to do the following:

- Implement a basic page with a single-button user interaction and manage its state using all three basic state management techniques.

- Differentiate between all three basic state management techniques.

Technical requirements

In order to successfully understand and execute everything explained in this chapter, you should have Flutter set up on your computer:

```
https://flutter.dev/docs/get-started/install
```

If you already have Flutter set up, make sure your version is at least *version 2*. To check your current version, go to **Terminal** (in **macOS**) or **Command Prompt** (in **Windows**) and run the following command:

```
flutter doctor
```

You can use any **IDE** that supports Flutter. Some well-known ones are **VSCode**, **Android Studio**, and **IntelliJ IDEA**.

All the code shown in this chapter is uploaded (in complete form) on **GitHub**:

```
https://github.com/PacktPublishing/Managing-State-in-Flutter-
Pragmatically/tree/main/ch2
```

Managing states within a widget with setState

This is the simplest approach you can use to change states inside your Flutter application whenever a user interacts with it. This uses a simple function call (known as `setState`) which, whenever called, rebuilds the widget (that is, runs the build method again) that you called the function in. This also rebuilds every other widget that is under that specific widget tree. A *widget tree* is something that contains widgets being built inside widgets. So, in the case where a widget rebuilds due to a user interaction, all the widgets inside it are also going to rebuild themselves. This section will also include an optional challenge where you will learn how to perform the optimized rebuilding of widgets.

The counter application example

Let's jump to the most basic example which uses `setState` to change states. This example can also be seen in the sample Flutter application which is created through the `flutter doctor` command.

If you have completed the Flutter set up on your computer using the previous link, create a new application through Terminal or Command Prompt by running the following command:

```
flutter create any_name_you_wish
```

This will create a whole new Flutter application in a folder you named. If you run this application, you will see the same screen we saw in *Figure 1.2* in *Chapter 1, States and State Management Overview*, which shows a counter being incremented on a button press. This is the application created by Flutter itself as a starting point for you.

Open the application code in your choice of IDE and open the `lib/main.dart` file. Here, you will see a lot of comments written by the Flutter team to help you as a beginner. As you have previously worked on Flutter, this should not be the first time you are seeing this file. In this file, you will see a function named `_incrementCounter`. Inside that function, you will see the `setState` function which is incrementing our counter for us. It looks something like this:

```
void _incrementCounter() {
    setState(() {
      _counter++;
    });
}
```

This `setState` function is a framework function provided by the Flutter team with every stateful widget.

> **Note**
>
> If you are not familiar with *stateful* and *stateless* widgets, please refer to the Flutter official documentation:
>
> `https://flutter.dev/docs/development/ui/interactive`

As you can see in the preceding code, this setState function takes a void callback function as its parameter. Inside that function, we tell setState what variable we need to update. As soon as this setState method is called, it rebuilds the current widget and the widgets that are inside it with all the updated values we put inside it.

Widget rebuilding – widget trees

As we just saw, the setState function rebuilds the widget that you are currently inside, along with widgets that are below it. So, let's try to understand what this means.

Create a new file in your lib folder, name it as my_stateful_widget.dart, and create the following stateful class inside that file:

```
import 'package:flutter/material.dart';

class ExampleStatefulPage extends StatefulWidget {
  @override
  _ExampleStatefulPageState createState() =>
    _ExampleStatefulPageState();
}

class _ExampleStatefulPageState extends
State<ExampleStatefulPage> {
  @override
  Widget build(BuildContext context) {
    print('Child Widget builds');
    return Container();
  }
}
```

This is the simplest stateful class which contains just one Container widget. You must have noticed a print statement that says Child widget builds. I have deliberately written that inside the build method of our new class, just to know when this class is building itself.

Now, to understand how widgets rebuild widgets within themselves, call ExampleStatefulPage inside your main.dart, just below the counter helper text widget. Your code should look something like this:

```
Text(
      '$_counter',
```

```
style: Theme.of(context).textTheme.headline4,
        ),
ExampleStatefulPage(), // new code
```

If you hot-reload your application now or hot-restart your application, you will see Child widget builds printing in your console log every time you press the increment counter button. This is because your parent widget is your main home page, and your child widget is ExampleStatefulPage, and the setState function is being called inside your parent class, therefore, it will rebuild itself, along with all of its children widgets.

You can also add a print statement inside your home page class to confirm that every button press reruns your build method of that specific widget.

With this little experiment, we now understand how the setState function works and how it builds a specific widget and all its descendants.

Passing data to another screen – setState example

We have seen how to update the values of variables shown in our screen through a setState function call. Now, let's see how we can pass our counter value to another screen using page constructors. We will also update the value in the second page and check if it is reflected in our first page.

We will use the same counter application that you created using the flutter create command:

1. Inside your lib folder, create a new dart file with the name page_two.dart. Add the following code to create a sample UI that will show the counter that is passed from the previous page:

```
import 'package:flutter/material.dart';

class PageTwo extends StatefulWidget {
  int counter;
  PageTwo({required this.counter});
  @override
  _PageTwoState createState() => _PageTwoState();
}


class _PageTwoState extends State<PageTwo> {
```

```
void _incrementCounter() {
  setState(() {
    widget.counter++;
  });
}
...

// Rest of the page is as the previous one with one
change in the body:
  Text(
'${widget.counter}', // updated code
style: Theme.of(context).textTheme.headline4,
  ),
...
```

This code is pretty much the same as the previous page. Instead of having the counter variable declared inside our class, we are fetching it from the constructor of the widget.

2. In order for this page to receive the counter from your main page, you need to update your `main.dart` file's `_incrementCounter` function as follows:

```
void _incrementCounter() {
  Navigator.of(context).push(
    MaterialPageRoute(
      builder: (context) => PageTwo(counter:
        _counter),
    ),
  );
}
```

Previously, we were setting our counter value inside this function. Now, we are simply navigating to `PageTwo` and passing our `_counter` value in its constructor.

3. Now, since our function does not increment anything, we better rename it `_navigate`:

```
void _navigate() {
  Navigator.of(context).push(
    MaterialPageRoute(
```

```
        builder: (context) => PageTwo(counter:
          _counter),
      ),
    );
  }
```

4. Lastly, update the default _counter value from 0 to 1 just for the sake of having a good argument to pass down to PageTwo:

    ```
    int _counter = 1;
    ```

Now, if you run the code, you will be able to navigate to page two by pressing the add button on the first screen. The second page should show the counter value as 1, and it should now increment your value every time you press the plus button. But you will notice that as soon as you go back to the previous screen, you will see the default value of your counter as 1 – the main page is not showing the updated counter value. Let's see how to solve this problem.

Updating the first screen's counter value

There are two ways (using only the things we have studied up until now) through which we can update our counter value on the first screen:

*   Using the pop() function from Navigator class
*   Using a callback

Let's first see how we can update the first screen using the pop() function:

1. In order to go back to the previous screen, Dart gives us the following piece of code, which can be used at any button press to navigate back:

    ```
    Navigator.of(context).pop();
    ```

    This line automatically navigates back to the previous page in the navigation stack. In PageTwo, this is currently happening automatically because the appBar property inside the Scaffold widget handles the back navigation for you if you don't put it in yourself (the back arrow in the app bar can be seen on the screen by default even if you don't write the code for it).

2. Change your AppBar inside PageTwo to look something like this:

    ```
    appBar: AppBar(
      title: Text('Page Two'),
    ```

```
   leading: IconButton(
     icon: Icon(Icons.arrow_back),
     onPressed: () {
       Navigator.of(context).pop(widget.counter);
     },
   ),
 )
```

The `AppBar` widget now has a leading widget that takes the place of the back arrow which was created automatically. There is one more thing that is amazing, and that is the `pop()` function having `widget.counter` as an argument. This argument tells the previous page in the navigation stack that *there is something that I want to send to you, that you need to receive it.*

3. To receive the counter value sent by `PageTwo`, we need to make some little changes to our code inside `main.dart`. Update your `_navigate` function to this:

```
void _navigate() async {
    var value = await Navigator.of(context).push(
      MaterialPageRoute(
        builder: (context) => PageTwo(counter:
          _counter),
      ),
    );
    if(value != null) setState(() {
      _counter= value;
    });
}
```

Whatever you put inside the `pop()` function in `PageTwo`, it will be returned as a return value here in this push function. So, this code now expects that after `PageTwo` is popped, it is going to return a value. This will be our counter value of course, and we set it to our `_counter` value in the current page using the `setState` function.

> **Note**
>
> If you are not familiar with the `async` and `await` keywords, please refer to the Flutter official documentation about asynchronous programming:
>
> `https://dart.dev/codelabs/async-await`

This was one way of getting our first page to know the latest counter value. Let's see the better way of doing this – that is, *callbacks* (the GitHub code has the callback already implemented).

Callbacks in Dart are used when you want to call a function declared in the parent class from within a child class. In our case, we want our updated counter value from `PageTwo` inside our main page. For that we will perform the following:

1. First, create a callback inside `PageTwo`. Introduce a new parameter inside your stateful class `PageTwo`:

```
class PageTwo extends StatefulWidget {
  final Function(int) callback;
  int counter;


  PageTwo({required this.counter, required
    this.callback});


  @override
  _PageTwoState createState() => _PageTwoState();
}
```

This function will be invoked by `PageTwo` every time the counter gets incremented.

2. So, let's add that invocation. Inside `_incrementCounter`, just below your `setState` call, add this callback:

```
void _incrementCounter() {
  setState(() {
    widget.counter++;
  });
  widget.callback(widget.counter); // new code
}
```

3. Let's see how to consume this callback in our `main.dart` file. Update your navigation code to something like this:

```
void _navigate() {
  Navigator.of(context).push(
    MaterialPageRoute(
      builder: (context) => PageTwo(
        counter: _counter,
```

```
        callback: (value) {
          setState(() {
            _counter = value;
          });
        },
      ),
    ),
  );
}
```

So, now you see we have one more parameter in the constructor of `PageTwo`. That parameter is a whole function, which is called whenever `PageTwo` calls it from inside. It brings with itself a new counter value, which is updated with our value inside `main.dart`. This is how values can be updated within pages using `setState`.

Section overview – setState

In this section, we learned the following:

- How to call a `setState` function to update variables inside your widget.
- How to pass down a variable to another screen.
- Two ways of how to keep the variable's value consistent in both pages.
- Using Push and Pop from Navigator to transfer data within pages.
- Using callbacks to update the counter value.
- The `setState` function reruns the build method of the current widget and all the widgets that are inside that.
- The `setState` function takes a void callback function as a parameter in which we update our variables with new values that we want the user to see.

The next section discusses inherited widgets and the inherited model. These are a combined form of state management that is written over `setState` functionality to provide some added feasibility and ease for managing states in your Flutter application.

Optional challenge – setState

Before we move on to the next section, here is a little optional challenge for you with `setState`.

You are to create three screens:

- Main page
- Screen A
- Screen B

The main page should have a `Text` widget showing the counter value (with the default set to `1`) and two buttons. Each button navigates to Screen A and Screen B respectively. screens A and B both have a `Text` widget showing the counter value they receive from the main page and a button for incrementing the counter.

Now for the challenge. Both screens A and B should be able to update the counter, and the latest updated counter value should be seen in all three screens.

Inherited widgets – injecting the state at the root

We observed that by using `setState` functionality we can tell the code which values to update. We also found out how to pass down the data within the widgets through constructors. This technique can turn into a real mess when you have a very deep widget hierarchy. You will have to pass down your counter value to every widget in order to be able to make it accessible by the deepest widget.

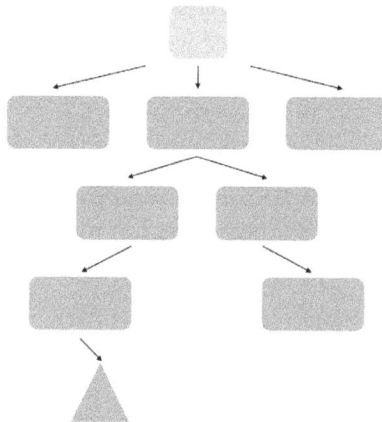

Figure 2.1 – Triangle widget trying to access counter value from the topmost square widget

In order to save the effort of passing the value down to every widget for accessibility, we have something called `InheritedWidget`. This inherited widget sits at the root of your widget tree and its values can be accessed using the `.of` method. You might have stumbled on something like `Theme.of(context).textTheme.title`. This is exactly what we will be doing with our counter example so that our counter value can be accessed using our context. Flutter uses this technique in its overall framework for passing down the theme data throughout your application.

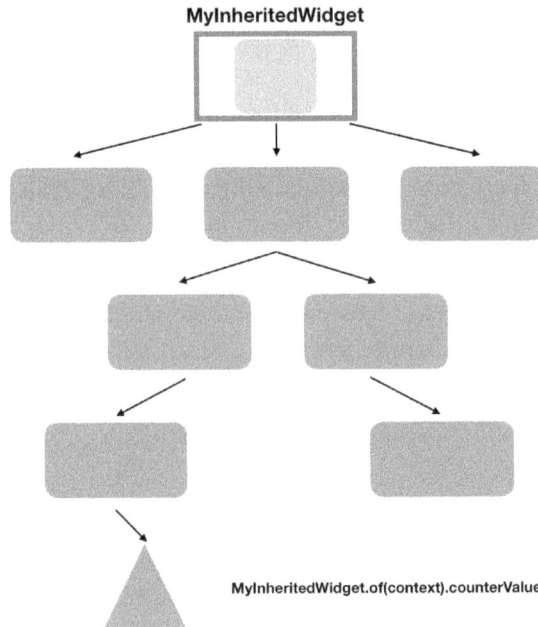

Figure 2.2 – InheritedWidget sits at the top in order to inject the state throughout the widget tree

Let's see the most basic implementation of passing our counter value down to our widget tree. Wrap your home page with an inherited widget like this:

> **Note**
> The code in the GitHub repository is the final implementation done by the end of the section – initially, the code might seem different.

```
MyInheritedWidget(
        child: MyHomePage(title: 'Flutter Demo Home Page'),
        counter: 1,
),
```

This will probably start giving you a compile time error because `MyInheritedWidget` doesn't exist. Let's create it:

```
class MyInheritedWidget extends InheritedWidget {
  const MyInheritedWidget({
    Key? key,
    required this.counter,
    required Widget child,
  }) : super(key: key, child: child);

  final int counter;

  static MyInheritedWidget of(BuildContext context) {
    final MyInheritedWidget? result =
    context.dependOnInheritedWidgetOfExactType
      <MyInheritedWidget>();
    assert(result != null, 'No counter found in context');
    return result!;
  }

  @override
  bool updateShouldNotify(MyInheritedWidget old) => counter
    != old.counter;
}
```

> **Note**
>
> If you aren't familiar with ? and ! notations, please refer to the official Flutter documentation regarding *sound null safety* (https://dart.dev/null-safety).

Your widget should extend `InheritedWidget`, which is provided in the Flutter framework. As soon as you extend `InheritedWidget`, it will ask you to override and implement a compulsory method, `updateShouldNotify`. This function is fired whenever anything inside your widget is updated. It checks the previous state and, if there is a change in state, this method returns `true`, which in turn rebuilds your widget tree.

Notice that we also have this static `.of` method. This is the function that is used with context to get the state within the widget tree. This function returns the state of the exact type of widget that we are looking for – in our case, it is `MyInheritedWidget`. We have a widget parameter that we will need in order to get our `InheritedWidget` to act as a wrapper around our main widget tree. Let's see how we get the counter value that we injected before:

```
Text(
  '${MyInheritedWidget.of(context).counter}',
)
```

If you look at this in a wider context, we can now access this counter variable anywhere below our main home page using this `.of` method. We don't need to pass the counter variable in page constructors as we did in the previous section of this chapter.

But this is just receiving and reading the counter variable. What if we want to update/increment the counter? We will have to create some more boilerplate code in order to do that.

> **Note**
> *Boilerplate* code is something that developers write in order to reuse code components and minimize redundant coding.

Inherited widgets – updating the counter variable

In order to update the counter variable, we will have to create some boilerplate code which is a combination of what we studied in `setState` along with what we studied just now regarding inherited widgets. So, let's create two important classes that we will need for our code to be able to update the counter. Create a file named `inherited_counter.dart` and add the code of both the following classes:

- `MyInheritedWidget` class
- `MyCounterWidget` stateful class

Here, `MyInheritedWidget` class is pretty simple:

```
class MyInheritedWidget extends InheritedWidget {
  final MyCounterInheritedWidgetState data;

  MyInheritedWidget({
    Key? key,
```

```
    required Widget child,
    required this.data,
  }) : super(key: key, child: child);

  @override
  bool updateShouldNotify(InheritedWidget oldWidget) =>
  child != oldWidget;
}
```

The same stuff that we are familiar with. This class has a property of
`MyCounterInheritedWidgetState`. This is going to be a wrapper for our internal
stateful class. Notice that this class doesn't have an `of` method. We are going to adjust that
in our stateful class:

```
class MyCounterInheritedWidget extends StatefulWidget {
  final Widget child;

  const MyCounterInheritedWidget({Key? key, required
    this.child})
      : super(key: key);

  static MyCounterInheritedWidgetState of(BuildContext
    context) {
    final MyCounterInheritedWidgetState? result =
        context.dependOnInheritedWidgetOfExactType
          <MyInheritedWidget>()!.data;

    assert(result != null, 'No counter found in context');
    return result!;
  }

  @override
  State<StatefulWidget> createState() {
    return MyCounterInheritedWidgetState();
  }
}
```

```
class MyCounterInheritedWidgetState extends
State<MyCounterInheritedWidget> {
  int _counterValue = 0;

  int get counterValue => _counterValue;

  void incrementCounter() {
    setState(() {
      _counterValue++;
    });
  }

  @override
  Widget build(BuildContext context) {
    return MyInheritedWidget(
      child: widget.child,
      data: this,
    );
  }
}
```

If you look at this stateful class carefully, you will see how it is using the static `of` method in its `MyCounterInheritedWidget` class and the `setState` method in the `MyCounterInheritedWidgetState` class. This is a kind of boilerplate code that is going to keep our counter variable for the rest of our application to access. It is going to call the `setState` method whenever the counter is incremented in order to tell all the widgets using the `.of` method to rebuild and read the new counter variable. The `MyCounterInheritedWidgetState` class wraps our inherited widget in order to be able to notify the application whenever the state of the counter is updated.

Let's see this code being used by our main application. Go back to your `main.dart` file and update the following code:

```
import 'package:flutter/material.dart';

import 'inherited_widget_counter.dart';

void main() {
  runApp(MyApp());
```

```
}

class MyApp extends StatelessWidget {
  @override
  Widget build(BuildContext context) {
    return MaterialApp(
      title: 'Flutter Demo',
      theme: ThemeData(
        primarySwatch: Colors.blue,
      ),
      home: MyCounterInheritedWidget(child:
        MyHomePage(title: 'Flutter Demo Home Page')),
    );
  }
}

class MyHomePage extends StatefulWidget {
  MyHomePage({Key? key, required this.title}) : super(key:
    key);

  final String title;

  @override
  _MyHomePageState createState() => _MyHomePageState();
}

class _MyHomePageState extends State<MyHomePage> {
  @override
  Widget build(BuildContext context) {
    return Scaffold(
      appBar: AppBar(
        title: Text('Title'),
      ),
      body: Center(
        child: Column(
          mainAxisAlignment: MainAxisAlignment.center,
```

```
              children: <Widget>[
                Text('Counter value:'),
                MyTextWidget(), // New widget
                MyButton(), // New widget
              ],
            ),
          ),
        );
    }
}


class MyTextWidget extends StatelessWidget {
  @override
  Widget build(BuildContext context) {
    print('Text widget builds');
    return Text(
      MyCounterInheritedWidget.of(context)
        .counterValue.toString(),
    );
  }
}


class MyButton extends StatelessWidget {
  @override
  Widget build(BuildContext context) {
    print('Button widget builds');
    return ElevatedButton(
      onPressed: () {
        MyCounterInheritedWidget.of(context)
          .incrementCounter();
      },
      child: Text('Add'),
    );
  }
}
```

Now, you will notice the difference in your main application's code. It's cleaner, without any `setState` calls or any counter variable being incremented. You just have two lines of code – one reads the counter from your inherited widget and the other increments the counter. Simple and clean. Also, it has the added benefit of not passing down the counter value in every widget we create.

> **Note**
> If you wish to get the updated counter value within navigations, you will have to wrap `MyCounterInheritedWidget` around your whole application. Currently, we have just wrapped it around one page, which when navigated to won't retain the state.

Section overview – inherited widgets

In this code-rich section, we learned the following about inherited widgets:

- Inherited widgets are used to pass down the state without having to put the variables in widget constructors.

- Inherited widgets, combined with `setState` functionality, can be very helpful in updating the state from anywhere in the application.

- With a little boilerplate code, we can have readable, good-looking, and clean code inside our main applications' widgets.

- We understand the use of static `.of` methods inside our self-created inherited widgets.

This section was all about inherited widgets. Now, let's look at a more refined version of inherited widgets used to optimize things for a larger application.

Inherited models – optimizing inherited widgets

If you add `print` statements in the `build` methods of `MyTextWidget` and `MyButton`, you will notice both getting printed every time the counter is incremented. However, the counter is updated only in `MyTextWidget` and `MyButton` has no use of the counter value. Wouldn't it be great if only those widgets which consume the value are rebuilt rather than every widget which is using the `.of` method? Inherited models to the rescue!

Inherited models are used in place of the inherited widget extension. These models provide the `aspect` value, which allows the provisioning of rebuilding the selected widgets and not the whole widget tree. Let's update our code a little in order to achieve what we expect.

`MyInheritedWidget` should now extend `InheritedModel<int>` instead of an `InheritedWidget`. As soon as you do that, it will ask you to override a compulsory method named `updateShouldNotifyDependent`. The overall class should now look something like this:

```
class MyInheritedWidget extends InheritedModel<int> {
  final MyCounterInheritedWidgetState data;

  MyInheritedWidget({
    Key? key,
    required Widget child,
    required this.data,
  }) : super(key: key, child: child);

  @override
  bool updateShouldNotify(InheritedWidget oldWidget) =>
    child != oldWidget;

  @override
  bool updateShouldNotifyDependent(
      covariant InheritedModel<int> oldWidget, Set<int>
        dependencies) {
    if (dependencies.contains(1)) return true;
    return false;
  }
}
```

This method is specifically returning `true` or `false` based on the aspects that it receives in the set of dependencies. Every dependent widget from the outside sends its own `aspect` and this function checks what aspects are to be rebuilt.

Inside `updateShouldNotifyDependent`, I have checked if the dependencies contain 1. I have kept this 1 as a reference to those widgets which listen to my counter variable. Therefore, all those with an `aspect` value of 1 are to be rebuilt whenever the counter is incremented. You will grasp this concept when we update our code inside our main widgets.

Update `MyTextWidget` in your `main.dart` file to this:

```
class MyTextWidget extends StatelessWidget {
  @override
  Widget build(BuildContext context) {
    print('Text widget builds');
    return Text(
      InheritedModel.inheritFrom
        <MyInheritedWidget>(context, aspect: 1)!
          .data
          .counterValue
          .toString(),
    );
  }
}
```

This is now fetching the counter value from the inherited model instead of the inherited widget (with an `aspect` value of 1). This means that this widget has told our inherited model to rebuild this specific widget whenever the counter increments.

Update the `MyButton` widget in your `main.dart` file to this:

```
class MyButton extends StatelessWidget {
  @override
  Widget build(BuildContext context) {
    print('Button widget builds');
    return ElevatedButton(
      onPressed: () {
        InheritedModel.inheritFrom
          <MyInheritedWidget>(context, aspect: 2)!
            .data
            .incrementCounter();
      },
      child: Text('Add'),
    );
  }
}
```

Here, we gave an `aspect` value of 2 so that this widget doesn't register itself for rebuilding during the update.

Now, if you run the application and increment the counter, you will see only `Text widget builds` being printed in the console, which is clearly very optimal in the case of larger applications where we might have a deep widget hierarchy and we want to prevent the unnecessary rebuilding of widgets.

Remember the optional challenge?

Now that you have learned about inherited widgets and inherited models, try that optional challenge again (the one at the end of the *Managing states within a widget with setState* section), but this time with inherited widgets and inherited models.

Section overview – inherited models

This section was about optimizing the idea of inherited widgets to make sure only certain widgets are rebuilt during a user interaction. In this section we learned the following:

- Inherited models use `aspect` values to determine which widgets to rebuild.
- `aspect` can be of any data type – in our case, we kept it as an integer.
- We saw two different widgets using the same inherited model, but only the real consumer of the counter value being rebuilt.
- Inherited models can be very effective in places where the widget hierarchy is deep and we want only certain widgets to rebuild to retain better performance.

Summary

We studied three major areas of basic state management in this chapter – the `setState` method, inherited widgets, and inherited models,

The `setState` method is the most basic form of state management, where, using a function provided by the Flutter framework, you can tell your code which values to update and rebuild your widgets accordingly. This technique rebuilds the whole main widget you are standing inside, along with all the widgets that are called inside your main widget. We also learned how to pass down your state using constructors, and pass back the values using the `pop` function and callbacks.

Inherited widgets come to the rescue by passing down the state deep within the widget hierarchy using constructors. The main inherited widget sits at the top of your widget hierarchy and passes the state down using the .of method. It uses context to make the state accessible to all the widgets down the widget tree.

Inherited models are an optimized version of inherited widgets where you can specifically rebuild certain widgets in your widget tree, more specifically, those that are actually consuming your state variables. Those that are responsible for only updating the state don't necessarily need to rebuild themselves (for example, a button with a static text). Inherited models use aspects to check which widgets need rebuilding and which do not.

In the next chapter, we are going to look into some well-known and advanced state management techniques, such as **BloC** and **Provider**, which internally use the concepts we have learned in this chapter.

Section 2: Types, Techniques, and Approaches

This section describes all the widely used state management approaches in detail, both those recommended by Google and those recommended by members of the developer community from around the world.

In this section, there are the following chapters:

- *Chapter 3, Diving into Advanced State Management Approaches*
- *Chapter 4, Adopting State Management Approaches from React*
- *Chapter 5, Executing Distinctive Approaches like GetX, GetIt, and Binder*

3
Diving into Advanced State Management Approaches

In the previous chapter, we learned how to create optimized screens that rebuild only the widgets required for user interaction. We also learned about two of the most basic and core implementations of state management techniques, which are `setState` and `InheritedWidget`.

In this chapter, we will study the two most popular state management techniques, which are **Provider** and **BLoC**, and their slight variations, **Riverpod** and **Cubit**, which make things easier for the developer. We will look at the following:

- **Provider** – an easier implementation of `InheritedWidget`
- **Riverpod** – a much easier version of Provider
- **BLoC** – business logic component
- **Cubit** – simplified BLoC

During your **Flutter** development journey, you are most likely going to use one of these techniques to build a state management solution for your application. So, it is highly recommended you understand each one of them deeply in order to decide which one is the most suited to your application. By the end of this chapter, you should be able to do the following:

- Understand how to implement a basic page with a single-button user interaction and manage its state using all of the state management approaches.

- Differentiate between all the state management approaches.

Technical requirements

In order to successfully understand and execute everything explained in this chapter, you should have Flutter set up on your computer:

`https://flutter.dev/docs/get-started/install`

If you already have Flutter set up, make sure your version is at least *version 2*. To check your current version, go to **Terminal** (in **macOS**) or **Command Prompt** (in **Windows**) and run the following command:

```
flutter doctor
```

You can use any **IDE** that supports Flutter. Some well-known ones are **VSCode**, **Android Studio**, and **IntelliJ IDEA**.

All the code shown in this chapter is uploaded (in complete form) on **GitHub**: `https://github.com/PacktPublishing/Managing-State-in-Flutter-Pragmatically/tree/main/ch3`.

Provider – using less boilerplate code than InheritedWidget

If you understood `InheritedWidget` well from the previous chapter, you will be able to grasp `Provider` much faster. This is due to the fact that `Provider` functions just the same as `InheritedWidget`, but with much less boilerplate code. You won't need to set up a separate inherited widget class and an intermediate class that uses `setState` functions within itself. You will only be using the `Provider` class wrapped around your root widget along with accessing it inside any of the children widgets using the `.of` method. Let's revisit this and try the same counter app example using `Provider`.

Adding a Provider dependency in a sample application

Create a new application using any name you want just like we did in the previous chapter:

```
flutter create any_name_you_wish
```

You will get the same counter example application with the default `setState` management technique implemented to update the counter value.

Let's see how to embed Provider into your application's code:

1. Open up a browser and go to `https://pub.dev/`.

2. Type `provider` in the search bar and hit *Enter*.

3. Click on the **provider** package that is most frequently used. It looks something like this:

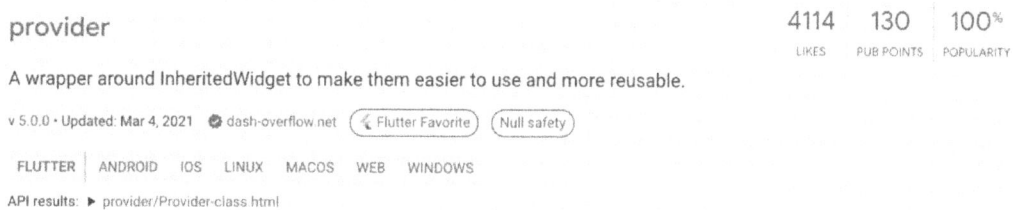

provider

	4114	130	100%
	LIKES	PUB POINTS	POPULARITY

A wrapper around InheritedWidget to make them easier to use and more reusable.

v 5.0.0 · Updated: Mar 4, 2021   ◆ dash-overflow.net   (⟨ Flutter Favorite)   (Null safety)

FLUTTER | ANDROID   IOS   LINUX   MACOS   WEB   WINDOWS

API results: ▶ provider/Provider-class.html

Figure 3.1 – Selecting the Provider package

A Reminder from the Previous Chapter

You can see the package description says "a wrapper around `InheritedWidget`." This means it uses the core functionality of `InheritedWidget` in order to provide easier functions for the developer to use with less boilerplate code.

---

4. When you are on the Provider package detail page, go to the **Installing** tab and copy the Provider package dependency, `provider: ^5.0.0` (the version may be different depending on the latest update).

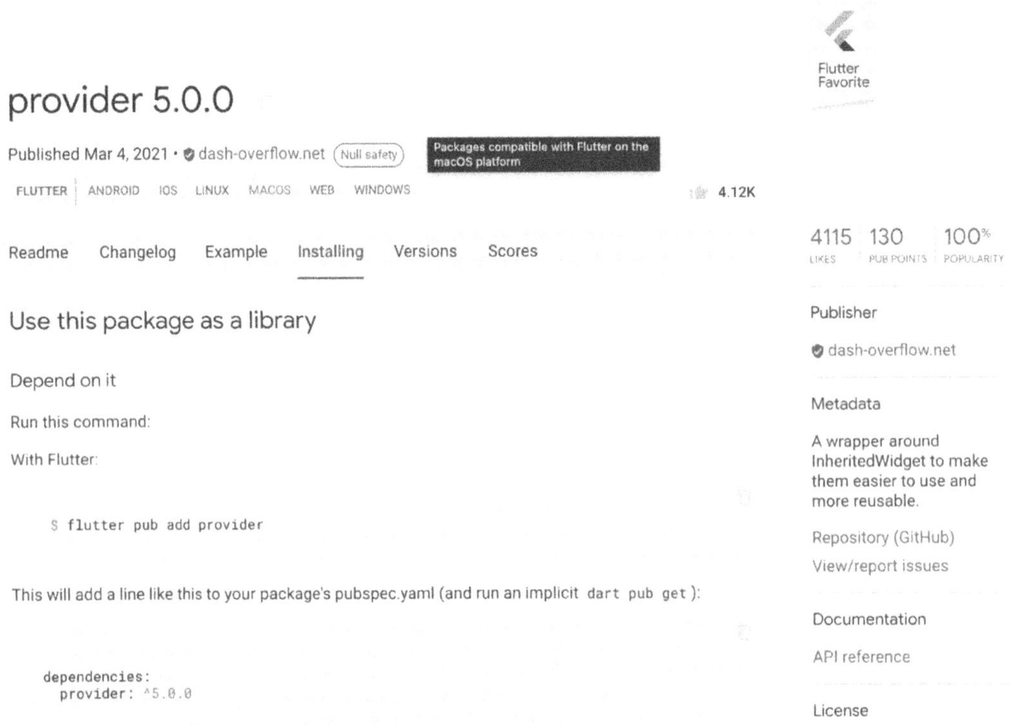

provider 5.0.0

Published Mar 4, 2021 · ✔ dash-overflow.net (Null safety) Packages compatible with Flutter on the macOS platform

FLUTTER | ANDROID   IOS   LINUX   MACOS   WEB   WINDOWS   ⌂ 4.12K

Readme   Changelog   Example   Installing   Versions   Scores

4115   130   100%
LIKES   PUB POINTS   POPULARITY

Use this package as a library

Depend on it

Run this command:

With Flutter:

```
$ flutter pub add provider
```

This will add a line like this to your package's pubspec.yaml (and run an implicit `dart pub get`):

```
dependencies:
  provider: ^5.0.0
```

Publisher

✔ dash-overflow.net

Metadata

A wrapper around InheritedWidget to make them easier to use and more reusable.

Repository (GitHub)

View/report issues

Documentation

API reference

License

Figure 3.2 – Installing the Provider package

5. Go to your code and open the `pubspec.yaml` file present in your root folder.

6. Find the `dependencies` header and add the `provider` dependency under it:

```
dependencies:
  flutter:
    sdk: flutter
  provider: ^5.0.0
```

7. Make sure you add the indents correctly. The `provider` package declaration should be underneath the `flutter` declaration, as shown in the preceding code example.

8. Your IDE should give a suggestion to run `flutter pub get` or `flutter packages get` in order to update the dependency that you just added. If not, you can open the terminal inside your IDE and type any of these two commands to update your dependency.

Now, you are ready to consume the code of this package inside your application.

Consuming Provider using the ChangeNotifierProvider class

As we learned in the previous chapter, we have to wrap the whole widget tree with `InheritedWidget` in order to access the states within every child. We are going to do the same with Provider but using `ChangeNotifierProvider`. If you go to the top of `main.dart`, you will see your main function that will be calling your main application, something like this:

```
runApp(MyApp());
```

Replace this code with the following:

```
runApp(
  ChangeNotifierProvider<Counter>(
    child: MyApp(),
    create: (_) => Counter(),
  ),
);
```

If you remember from the previous chapter, there was some boilerplate code that we wrote in order to make `InheritedWidget` work, and all of that boilerplate code is now embedded inside `ChangeNotifierProvider`. This is a type of Provider that takes a class as a type argument in triangular brackets and creates an instance of that class in the `create` parameter, as shown in the preceding example. For us, this `Counter` class doesn't exist yet, so let's create it. Create a new file named `provider_counter.dart` and add this `Counter` class inside it:

```
class Counter with ChangeNotifier {
  int _count = 0;

  void increment() {
    _count++;
    notifyListeners();
  }
}
```

We have two keywords that are new to us in the preceding code. `ChangeNotifier` is a mixin that we added to our class so that we can notify every child throughout our application of any changes that happen to this counter value. In order to notify, we have a function called `notifyListeners`. This function acts as `setState` for us.

> **Note**
>
> In order to know more about what a mixin is, please refer to **Dart**'s official documentation:
>
> `https://dart.dev/guides/language/language-tour#adding-features-to-a-class-mixins`

Since we have now wrapped our application in a Provider, we can access the state using the `.of(context)` method.

First, delete the `_MyHomePageState` class inside the `main.dart` file. Also, update your home option inside the `MyApp` class to not take `title` as an argument, as shown next:

```
class MyApp extends StatelessWidget {
  // This widget is the root of your application
  @override
  Widget build(BuildContext context) {
    return MaterialApp(
      title: 'Flutter Demo',
      theme: ThemeData(
        primarySwatch: Colors.blue,
      ),
      home: MyHomePage(), // title arg removed
    );
  }
}
```

Next, inside `provider_counter.dart`, add a class named `ProviderCounterExamplePage`, below the `Counter` class, with the following code inside it:

```
class ProviderCounterExamplePage extends StatelessWidget {
  @override
```

```dart
  Widget build(BuildContext context) {
    return Scaffold(
      appBar: AppBar(
        title: Text('Hello'),
      ),
      body: Center(
        child: Column(
          mainAxisAlignment: MainAxisAlignment.center,
          children: <Widget>[
            Text(
              'You have pushed the button this many
                times:',
            ),
            Text('${Provider.of<Counter>(context)._count}',
                style: Theme.of(context)
                  .textTheme.headline4),
          ],
        ),
      ),
      floatingActionButton: FloatingActionButton(
        onPressed: () =>
            Provider.of<Counter>(context, listen:
              false).increment(),
        tooltip: 'Increment',
        child: Icon(Icons.add),
      ),
    );
  }
}
```

`Provider.of<Counter>(context)._count` provides you with the ability to listen to the changes made to the counter every time the increment function is called. This looks similar to what we did in the previous chapter – the only difference is we have less boilerplate code now.

Similarly, `Provider.of<Counter>(context, listen: false).increment()` provides the ability to call the increment function we have in our `Counter` class. If you remember from the previous chapter, we explored the concept of *aspects*, which allow us to prevent the rebuilding of widgets that don't require reading the values of our variables. We have a similar concept here, with a much better and more readable implementation, called the `listen` parameter. And Provider requires this parameter to be set as `false` if you are only using it to call a method and not for reading values.

Now, if you run your application, you will have almost no boilerplate code and a better, more readable implementation for reading and updating values inside your main application's code. You can also use `context.watch<Counter>()._count` and `context.read<Counter>().increment()` instead of `Provider.of<Counter>(context)._count` and `Provider.of<Counter>(context, listen: false).increment()` respectively.

As we have wrapped our whole application in a `Provider` widget, we can access the state from anywhere in the application now. If we extract a separate widget for the counter text, we can still access the counter value using the `context` keyword:

```
class MyText extends StatelessWidget {
  @override
  Widget build(BuildContext context) {
    return Text('${context.watch<Counter>()._count}',
        style: Theme.of(context).textTheme.headline4);
  }
}
```

After using the preceding code in our main code, it should look something like this:

```
Text(
    'You have pushed the button this many times:',
),
MyText(),
```

Now, if you write `print` statements in both your classes, you will notice that only the `MyText` class rebuilds every time the increment is called. This particular way of creating separate widgets for independent small tasks is very handy when you are building large-scale applications.

Section overview – Provider

In this section, we learned the following:

- `Provider` is a wrapper around `InheritedWidget`.

- Provider is a Dart package that provides all required functionality and keeps the boilerplate code inside itself.

- Provider reduces the boilerplate code needed to be written when implementing `InheritedWidget`.

- Wrapping `Provider` around the application makes the state accessible in all the widgets.

- `Provider.of<YourClass>(context)` has a parameter named `listen`, which can be used to stop rebuilding widgets that don't read values from the class.

- `Provider.of<Counter>(context)._count` is similar to `context.watch<Counter>()._count`.

- `Provider.of<Counter>(context, listen: false).increment()` is similar to `context.read<Counter>().increment()`.

The next section is about Riverpod, which is an improvement to Provider. In principle, Riverpod uses concepts from Provider but with some enhancements and improved ease of use.

Riverpod – enhancing Provider

As Flutter frameworks got better with time, state management packages were also enhanced, and problems caused by older techniques were solved in newer ones. Riverpod is an enhancement of the `Provider` package. It uses the concepts of Provider underneath and adds to the functionality by providing improved flexibility and performance. One major problem that Riverpod solved was having the possibility of reading null objects from the states. Reading objects in Riverpod is now compile-safe, so you are always sure that you won't get a null when reading objects from states using `read` or `watch` functions. You can read more about Riverpod and its documentation on its official website at `https://riverpod.dev/`.

In this section, you are going to learn how to consume a `Riverpod` package inside your counter example application. You will also learn some new keywords that would be similar to the functionality discussed in the previous section.

Adding a Riverpod dependency in a sample application

Just like before, create a new Flutter application through the command line:

```
flutter create any_name_you_wish
```

You will get the same counter example application with the default `setState` management technique implemented to update the counter value.

Let's see how to embed Riverpod into your application's cod:.

1. Open up a browser and go to `https://pub.dev/`.

2. Type `riverpod` in the search bar and hit *Enter*.

3. You will find multiple packages related to Riverpod. We will be using `flutter_riverpod`. If you wonder why not `riverpod`, the reason is the `riverpod` package is used for Dart only and not for Flutter apps.

4. Go to the **Installing** tab (as we did in the previous section) and copy the `flutter_riverpod` package dependency, `flutter_riverpod: ^0.14.0+3` (the version may be different depending on the latest update).

flutter_riverpod 0.14.0+3

Published Apr 29, 2021 (Null safety)

FLUTTER | ANDROID IOS LINUX MACOS WEB WINDOWS   👍 392

Readme   Changelog   Example   Installing   Versions   Scores

Use this package as a library

Depend on it

Run this command:

With Flutter:

```
$ flutter pub add flutter_riverpod
```

This will add a line like this to your package's pubspec.yaml (and run an implicit dart pub get):

```
dependencies:
    flutter_riverpod: ^0.14.0+3
```

392   130   98%
LIKES   PUB POINTS   POPULARITY

Metadata

A simple way to access state from anywhere in your application while robust and testable.

Homepage

Repository (GitHub)

View/report issues

Documentation

API reference

Uploader

darky12s@gmail.com

Figure 3.3 – Installing the Riverpod package

5. Go to your code and open the `pubspec.yaml` file present in your root folder.

6. Find the `dependencies` header and add the `flutter_riverpod` dependency under it:

```
dependencies:
  flutter:
    sdk: flutter
  flutter_riverpod: ^0.14.0+3
```

7. Make sure you add the indents correctly. The `flutter_riverpod` package declaration should be underneath the `flutter` declaration, as shown in the preceding code example.

8. Your IDE should give a suggestion to run `flutter pub get` or `flutter packages get` in order to update the dependency that you just added. If not, you can open the terminal inside your IDE and type any of these two commands to update your dependency.

Let's consume `riverpod` in our example application to convert our counter example from `setState` to `riverpod`.

> **Note**
> The GitHub link has separate files named `riverpod_counter_simple.dart` and `riverpod_counter_custom.dart` for both simple and custom versions of updating the counter value, both of which are discussed next.

Using the simplest version of Riverpod to update the counter value

Let's begin with creating a bare minimum version of our counter example using the `Riverpod` package that we just added to our application. We will implement this in four precise steps:

1. Wrapping your application in the `ProviderScope` widget. This is similar to `ChangeNotifierProvider`, which we studied in the previous section.

2. Creating a global Provider. In `Riverpod`, every Provider is declared globally in order to make it easy to access the state from anywhere in the application.

3. Consuming the counter value in our UI code.

4. Incrementing the counter through the global Provider.

We begin by wrapping our application in the `ProviderScope` widget:

```
void main() {
    runApp(const ProviderScope(child: MyApp()));
}
```

Make sure to include the import at the top:

```
import 'package:flutter_riverpod/flutter_riverpod.dart'; // new
code
```

We will now create a global Provider in order to keep the state accessible everywhere in our application:

```
final counterProvider = StateProvider((ref) => 0);
```

This is the basic syntax for creating a global Provider using Riverpod state management. This line of code creates a state of the `int` type. It infers the type automatically as we return zero as an integer inside the callback function. Zero is the default value of this state but you can write any number you want your application counter to begin with.

Now, we add a `Consumer` widget, which allows us to listen to the state from Riverpod state management:

```
body: Center(
    child: Consumer(builder: (context, watch, _) {
        final count = watch(counterProvider).state;
        return Text('$count');
    }),
),
```

Notice the `Consumer` widget has a function call with parameters such as `context` and `watch`. This is simply another way of writing `context.watch<Counter>()._count`, which we studied in the previous section using Provider. Here, the `watch` function directly takes the global Provider as its input, which extracts the integer value from the state (which, by default, is zero).

For the last and most simple step, we increment the counter using something that we have been seeing a lot in this chapter, by updating `onPressed` inside `FloatingActionButton`:

```
onPressed: () => context.read(counterProvider).state++,
```

This is quite similar to what we did in the previous section. The only difference is the `read` function directly takes the global Provider as its input parameter and returns the state, which is of the `int` type. We increment the state directly using the `++` operator – the `watch` function in the main UI body listens to the change and updates the UI with an incremented counter value.

Your completed `riverpod_counter_simple.dart` file should look something like this:

```
import 'package:flutter/material.dart';
import 'package:flutter_riverpod/flutter_riverpod.dart';


final counterProvider = StateProvider((ref) => 0);


class RiverpodCustomCounterExample extends StatelessWidget {
  @override
  Widget build(BuildContext context) {
    return Scaffold(
      appBar: AppBar(title: const Text('Riverpod simple
      counter example')),
      body: Center(
        child: Consumer(builder: (context, watch, _) {
          final count = watch(counterProvider);
          return Text('$count');
        }),
      ),
      floatingActionButton: FloatingActionButton(
        onPressed: () => context.read(
        counterProvider).state++,
        child: const Icon(Icons.add),
      ),
    );
  }
}
```

This was a basic example of using a counter value inside our application using Riverpod. Let's say we want to have a class of our own and want to update the values of the properties inside that class. This takes us to `Notifier` and `StateNotifierProvider`.

Using a custom class as a state in Riverpod

While studying Riverpod for the first time, I came to the point where I had to have my own class of properties that I could update using Riverpod state management. This led me to explore `Notifier` and `StateNotifierProvider`. Let's look at the code and understand how they work:

1. Update your global Provider declaration to this:

```
final counterProvider = StateNotifierProvider((ref) =>
CounterNotifier());
```

There are two updates here:

a. The return type is `CounterNotifier` instead of zero now.

b. `StateProvider` is updated to `StateNotifierProvider`.

2. Create a `CounterNotifier` class, which is a type of `StateNotifier`:

```
class CounterNotifier extends StateNotifier<CounterModel>
{
    CounterNotifier() : super(CounterModel(count: 0));

    void increment() => state = CounterModel(count:
        state.count + 1);
}
```

Our provider is now `StateNotifierProvider`, so whatever class we assign it, it should be a type of `StateNotifier`. This is the reason our `CounterNotifier` class is extending `StateNotifier` of the `CounterModel` type.

3. This `CounterModel` is our custom class where we can keep as many properties and functions as we want. For now, we are going with a single counter value along with its increment function, for the sake of this example:

```
class CounterModel {
    int count;

    CounterModel({required this.count});
}
```

4. Since we have all the updates for our custom class in place, let's tweak our UI code to adjust to these changes:

```
child: Consumer(
  builder: (context, watch, _) {
    final state = watch(counterProvider) as
    CounterModel;
    return Text('${state.count}');
  },
),
```

Instead of directly accessing the state, we now typecast it into our custom class type and access the count property.

5. The `onPressed` function now looks like this:

```
onPressed: () => context.read(counterProvider.notifier).
increment(),
```

Instead of reading the global Provider directly, we now read the notifier and access the increment function we implemented. This opens up a lot of possibilities of creating our own methods and properties inside our custom class and accessing them through global providers using notifiers.

Now, the completed `riverpod_counter_custom.dart` file using custom class implementation should look something like this:

```
import 'package:flutter/material.dart';
import 'package:flutter_riverpod/flutter_riverpod.dart';


final counterProvider = StateNotifierProvider((ref) =>
CounterNotifier());

class CounterNotifier extends StateNotifier<CounterModel> {
  CounterNotifier() : super(CounterModel(count: 0));

  void increment() => state = CounterModel(count: state.count +
1);
}
```

```
class CounterModel {
  int count;

  CounterModel({required this.count});
}


class RiverpodCustomCounterExample extends StatelessWidget {
  @override
  Widget build(BuildContext context) {
    return Scaffold(
      appBar: AppBar(title: const Text('Riverpod custom
      counter example')),
      body: Center(
        child: Consumer(
          builder: (context, watch, _) {
            final state = watch(counterProvider) as
            CounterModel;
            return Text('${state.count}');
          },
        ),
      ),
      floatingActionButton: FloatingActionButton(
        onPressed: () => context.read(
        counterProvider.notifier).increment(),
        child: const Icon(Icons.add),
      ),
    );
  }
}
```

Using this technique, you can create as many providers and custom classes as you want and swiftly manage your properties in your application.

Section overview – Riverpod

In this section, we learned the following things about Riverpod:

- Riverpod is an enhancement to Provider state management.

- Riverpod is compile-safe for reading state values.

- Unlike Provider, the application is wrapped in a `ProviderScope` widget instead of a `ChangeNotifierProvider` widget.

- Providers are created globally in order to access the state everywhere in the application.

- We were introduced to a new widget called `Consumer`.

- We were introduced to `StateNotifier` and `StateNotifierProvider`.

- We saw how to add a custom class to manipulate properties and methods of our own choice.

The next section is about BLoC. This is one of the widely used state management techniques where you write the business logic of every component inside your application separately, which is tightly coupled to your UI classes.

BLoC – writing business logic separately

BLoC stands for **business logic component**. This technique is widely used in a lot of applications due to its capability of decoupling your core business logic from your UI, network, or repository classes. BLoC works on streams underneath and allows you to send events from your UI and receive states to your UI in order to update the changes based on user interaction. Inside BLoC state management, there are three main keywords you will have to get yourself familiarized with:

- The **bloc** itself (all your business logic lies inside this class)

- The **state** (this tells the UI when to update itself)

- The **event** (you trigger the events from your UI class in order to do something inside your bloc)

Adding a BLoC dependency in your application

Just like before, create a new Flutter application through the command line:

```
flutter create any_name_you_wish
```

You will get the same counter example application with the default `setState` management technique implemented to update the counter value.

Let's see how to embed BLoC into your application cod:.

1. Open up a browser and go to `https://pub.dev/`.

2. Type `bloc` in the search bar and hit *Enter*.

3. You will find multiple packages related to BLoC. We will be using `flutter_bloc`. The `bloc` package was made earlier for Dart and ported to Flutter afterward. The `flutter_bloc` package was made over `bloc` in order to make things easier.

4. Go to the **Installing** tab (as we did in the previous section) and copy the `flutter_bloc` package dependency, `flutter_bloc:  ^7.0.1` (the version may be different depending on the latest update).

Flutter
Favorite

flutter_bloc 7.0.1

Published May 29, 2021 • ⬤ bloclibrary.dev (Null safety)

FLUTTER | ANDROID   IOS   LINUX   MACOS   WEB   WINDOWS   2.32K

Readme   Changelog   Example   Installing   Versions   Scores

| 2321 | 130 | 99% |
| LIKES | PUB POINTS | POPULARITY |

Use this package as a library

Depend on it

Run this command:

With Flutter:

```
$ flutter pub add flutter_bloc
```

This will add a line like this to your package's pubspec.yaml (and run an implicit dart pub get):

```
dependencies:
    flutter_bloc: ^7.0.1
```

Publisher

⬤ bloclibrary.dev

Metadata

Flutter Widgets that make it easy to implement the BLoC (Business Logic Component) design pattern. Built to be used with the bloc state management package.

Homepage
Repository (GitHub)
View/report issues

Documentation

Figure 3.4 – Installing flutter_bloc

5.   Go to your code and open the `pubspec.yaml` file present in your root folder.

6.   Find the `dependencies` header and add the `flutter_bloc` dependency under it:

```
dependencies:
  flutter:
    sdk: flutter
  flutter_bloc: ^7.0.1
```

7.   Make sure you add the indents correctly. The `flutter_bloc` package declaration should be underneath the `flutter` declaration, as shown in the preceding code example.

8.   Your IDE should give a suggestion to run `flutter pub get` or `flutter packages get` in order to update the dependency that you just added. If not, you can open the terminal inside your IDE and type any of these two commands to update your dependency.

Let's consume `flutter_bloc` in our example application to convert our counter example from `setState` to BLoC.

Creating a counter example application using BLoC

As we have done with all other state management techniques, let's do the same for this one as well. We are going to turn our counter example application from `setState` to BLoC. We will be doing this in a number of steps:

1.   Creating state classes

2.   Creating event classes

3.   Creating a bloc class

4.   Consuming the bloc class in our UI

5.   Wrapping our main application with `BlocProvider`

The following figure might help you understand a high-level approach of using BLoC:

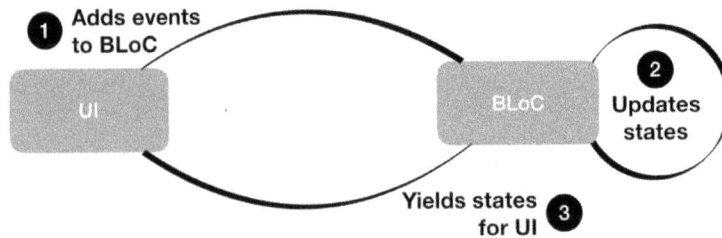

Figure 3.5 – High-level BLoC architecture

Creating classes for states and events

Let's create state classes and event classes first. For this, create a new file named counter_state.dart and add the following code:

```
import 'package:equatable/equatable.dart';


class CounterState extends Equatable {
    final int count;


    CounterState({this.count = 0});


    @override
    List<Object?> get props => [this.count];
}
```

This code will give errors related to the equatable package. This equatable package is a Flutter package that is used to compare whole objects with each other using the == operator. Otherwise, you will have to override the == operator for comparing different object types.

Add the package dependency from the package's website (https://pub.dev/packages/equatable) into your pubspec.yaml file just like we did with the flutter_bloc dependency.

Another thing that might be new for you is the overridden props property. This is a list in which you include all those properties that will be required in order to make this whole class equal to another class of the same type.

We also have a simple count property that will keep our counter value (default to zero), which will be shown on our screen.

Let's create the event class. Create a new file named `counter_event.dart` and add the following code:

```
class CounterEvent {}


class IncrementCounterEvent extends CounterEvent {}


class AddToCounterEvent extends CounterEvent {
  final int number;
  AddToCounterEvent({required this.number});
}
```

This file is pretty simple. We have a base class named `CounterEvent` and the other two classes extend this base class. `IncrementCounterEvent` will be fired from the UI if we want to increment one to our counter value, and `AddToCounterEvent` will be fired if we want to add a specific number to the counter. I have added this second event just to help you understand the idea of how events are handled in the BLoC file.

Creating our BLoC class

Now, let's see what our BLoC file looks like. Create a new file named `counter_bloc.dart` inside your `lib` directory and add the following code:

```
import 'counter_event.dart';
import 'package:flutter_bloc/flutter_bloc.dart';


import 'counter_state.dart';


class CounterBloc extends Bloc {
  CounterBloc() : super(initialState);

  static get initialState => CounterState();

  int countValue = 0;

  @override
  Stream mapEventToState(event) async* {
    if(event is IncrementCounterEvent) {
      yield CounterState(count: ++countValue);
```

```
    }
  if(event is AddToCounterEvent) {
    countValue = countValue + event.number;
    yield CounterState(count: countValue);
  }
 }
}
```

There are a few things to understand in this class:

- Our `CounterBloc` class extends `Bloc`, which is coming from the `flutter_ bloc` package.

- When we extend any class with `Bloc`, it becomes necessary to implement the `mapEventToState` function in order to receive events from the UI. This function is fired every time we add an event from our UI class.

- The return type of this function is `Stream`. At the beginning of this section, we discussed that BLoC works on streams, so whenever a state is updated, it is yielded inside this function. The listener of this `CounterBloc` class gets notified that a state has been updated.

- We can check for events using the `is` keyword, which acts like the `==` operator. Here is how `equatable` concepts come in.

- The initial state of our `CounterBloc` class is set to `CounterState()`, which has a default count value of zero.

- We store a `countValue` property inside our `CounterBloc` class in order to keep the state intact throughout the application life cycle.

Finalizing our UI code

We have now created all the necessary classes in order for our BLoC implementation to work. We just need to enable our UI to add events and listen to the state changes inside the `main.dart` file. We will first need to complete the following:

1. Wrap our `Text` widget inside a `BlocBuilder` widget, which will enable us to listen to the state changes:

```
BlocBuilder(
  bloc: BlocProvider.of<CounterBloc>(context),
  builder: (context, snapshot) {
```

```
    return Text(
      '${(snapshot as CounterState).count}',
      style: Theme.of(context).textTheme.headline4,
    );
  },
)
```

Make sure to import at the top:

```
import 'counter_bloc.dart';
import 'counter_event.dart';
import 'package:flutter/material.dart';
import 'package:flutter_bloc/flutter_bloc.dart';
```

`BlocBuilder` is a similar widget for BLoC as `Consumer` was for Riverpod. It allows us to listen to the changes and capture states. `BlocBuilder` has two main properties:

a. The first one is `bloc:`, which is quite self-explanatory and demands a valid BLoC class from the context hierarchy. We provide `BlocProvider. of<CounterBloc>(context)` to this property in order to make our text widget listen to `CounterBloc`. This line is similar to what we did in Provider and Riverpod in previous examples.

b. The other property is `builder`. This is where you get all the state changes and you can pick up the count value from within a state that is yielded by our `CounterBloc` class.

2. The `onPressed` function of your increment button, `FloatingActionButton`, should now look something like this:

```
onPressed: () {
  BlocProvider.of<CounterBloc>(context)
  .add(IncrementCounterEvent());
}
```

You can see we just added our `IncrementCounterEvent` function call in our BLoC instance. This is going to trigger the `mapEventToState` function in our `CounterBloc` class and we will have our state updated to an incremented counter value, which will be caught by the `BlocBuilder` widget we used in the preceding code.

3. We can also add the other event we created that was responsible for adding a specific number to the counter. This will require no further changes to the UI or our `BlocBuilder` widget and we will see that our counter now increments 4 seamlessly:

```
onPressed: () {
  BlocProvider.of<CounterBloc>(context)
  .add(AddToCounterEvent(number: 4));
}
```

This will add 4 to the counter value every time we press the button. Creating events, states, and BLoC classes separately enables us to have fewer changes in our UI classes if we only need to change how our business logic behaves.

Your completed `main.dart` class should look something like this:

```
import 'counter_bloc.dart';
import 'package:flutter/material.dart';
import 'package:flutter_bloc/flutter_bloc.dart';

import 'counter_event.dart';
import 'counter_state.dart';

void main() {
  runApp(MyApp());
}

class MyApp extends StatelessWidget {
  @override
  Widget build(BuildContext context) {
    return MultiBlocProvider(
      providers: [
        BlocProvider<CounterBloc>(
          create: (context) => CounterBloc(),
        ),
      ],
      child: MaterialApp(
        title: 'Flutter Demo',
        theme: ThemeData(
```

```
            primarySwatch: Colors.blue,
          ),
        home: MyHomePage(),
      ),
    );
  }
}

class MyHomePage extends StatelessWidget {
  @override
  Widget build(BuildContext context) {
    return Scaffold(
      appBar: AppBar(
        title: Text('Hello'),
      ),
      body: Center(
        child: Column(
          mainAxisAlignment: MainAxisAlignment.center,
          children: <Widget>[
            Text(
              'You have pushed the button this many
              times:',
            ),
            BlocBuilder(
              bloc: BlocProvider.of<CounterBloc>
              (context),
              builder: (context, snapshot) {
                return Text(
                  '${(snapshot as
                  CounterState).count}',
                  style: Theme.of(context
                  ).textTheme.headline4,
                );
              },
            ),
          ],
```

```
        ),
      ),
      floatingActionButton: FloatingActionButton(
        onPressed: () {
          BlocProvider.of<CounterBloc>(context)
          .add(IncrementCounterEvent());
        },
        child: Icon(Icons.add),
      ),
    );
  }
}
```

4. The final thing is to wrap our application in a `BlocProvider` widget or a `MultiBlocProvider` widget:

```
void main() {
  runApp(MyApp());
}

class MyApp extends StatelessWidget {
  @override
  Widget build(BuildContext context) {
    return MultiBlocProvider(
      providers: [
        BlocProvider<CounterBloc>(
          create: (context) => CounterBloc(),
        ),
      ],
      child: MaterialApp(
        title: 'Flutter Demo',
        theme: ThemeData(
          primarySwatch: Colors.blue,
        ),
        home: BlocCounterExample(),
```

```
        ),
      );
    }
  }
```

We wrapped our application in `MultiBlocProvider` in order to extend our application's functionality to have more BLoC classes in the future. Right now, we only have `CounterBloc` declared here so that we can get a valid, non-null instance of `CounterBloc` when we access it through `BlocProvider.of<CounterBloc>(context)`.

Optional challenge – BLoC

Here is an optional challenge for you:

1. Use two separate BLoC classes coupled to two different screens with two different counter values.

2. One BLoC class increments the counter value normally, the second increments it in multiples of `10`.

3. Create a third screen where both counter values (updated) are displayed.

Section overview – BLoC

In this section, we learned the following about BLoC:

- BLoC stands for business logic component.

- BLoC enables us to decouple our business logic from our UI.

- BLoC works on streams.

- We have events, states, and extended bloc classes while using BLoC.

- `equatable` is a package that allows us to compare object types wholly.

- `MultiBlocProvider` enables us to wrap multiple blocs to our application.

- Events are added to BLoC by the UI and states are yielded to the UI by BLoC.

The next section is about Cubit, which is a subset of BLoC. Cubit is usually used for simpler states because it doesn't use events. Rather, it uses simple functions to emit states. Let's see how to use Cubit in our counter example application.

Cubit – simplified BLoC

Cubit is a subset of the BLoC library and it is widely used where states are less complex. It has no events, and states are triggered using functions directly from the UI. This creates less complicated code for simpler user flows. Let's see how our counter example application looks with Cubit in place (you won't need to add any extra package other than `flutter_bloc` for using Cubit).

Creating a counter example application using Cubit

Most of the things in Cubit are going to be the same as they were in BLoC. We will be using the same state class that we used in BLoC, which is `CounterState`. We won't have any event class for Cubit – we will have a Cubit class. So, let's create a file named `counter_cubit.dart` and add the following code:

```
import 'counter_state.dart';
import 'package:flutter_bloc/flutter_bloc.dart';

class CounterCubit extends Cubit<CounterState> {
  CounterCubit() : super(initialState);

  static get initialState => CounterState();

  int countValue = 0;

  increment() async {
    emit(CounterState(count: ++countValue));
  }

  addNumberToCounter(int counter) async {
    countValue = countValue + counter;
    emit(CounterState(count: countValue));
  }
}
```

As you can see, in Cubit we have similar things to what we had in our BLoC class in the previous section. The few differences we can notice are as follows:

- Our `CounterCubit` class extends from a Cubit class. The `Cubit` class takes the state class as a type parameter in triangular brackets (`<>`).

- There is no mapEventToState function. Both the functions are directly created inside this Cubit class and will be called directly from the UI.

- Instead of yield, we have a function called emit(), which takes our state as a parameter and does the same thing as yield did in BLoC. It streams the result of the state to the UI class.

Create a copy of the MyHomePage class from the BLoC section. In our MyHomePage class, we have very small tweaks. The BlocBuilder part remains the same – we just have our CounterCubit class instead of the CounterBloc class inside the BLoC definition:

```
BlocBuilder(
  bloc: BlocProvider.of<CounterCubit>(context), // changed
  builder: (context, snapshot) {
    return Text(
      '${(snapshot as CounterState).count}',
      style: Theme.of(context).textTheme.headline4,
    );
  },
)
```

The onPressed function now calls the increment function directly instead of adding the event to BLoC:

```
onPressed: () {
  BlocProvider.of<CounterCubit>(context).increment();
}
```

Our Cubit class is wrapped around our application just like we had with BLoC:

```
void main() {
  runApp(MyApp());
}


class MyApp extends StatelessWidget {
  @override
  Widget build(BuildContext context) {
    return MultiBlocProvider(
      providers: [
        BlocProvider<CounterCubit>( //changed
```

```
            create: (context) => CounterCubit(), // changed
          ),
        ],
      child: MaterialApp(
        title: 'Flutter Demo',
        theme: ThemeData(
          primarySwatch: Colors.blue,
        ),
        home: CubitCounterExample(),
      ),
    );
  }
}
```

Section overview – Cubit

You must have noticed that Cubit's implementation is pretty similar to that of BLoC, therefore, Cubit is called a subset of BLoC. It is simple, straightforward, and can also be used with BLoC implementation in certain conditions.

Summary

This was a long chapter, detailing the most important and feature-rich implementations of state management techniques. We have learned four major state management techniques and their concepts and created our counter example application using all of them sequentially. The following major points can be taken away from this chapter:

- Provider is an extension and a wrapper over the InheritedWidget class, which uses .of(context) to access the states down the widget hierarchy.

- Riverpod is an enhanced version of Provider, where performance and flexibility were improved and a compile-safe feature was introduced.

- We studied BLoC – a different paradigm of state management that works on streams, events, and states. It is a widely used technique and decouples our UI from our business logic.

- Lastly, we studied Cubit, which is a subset of BLoC with no events and with simplified code inside the Cubit class.

In the next chapter, we will be studying state management approaches that were adopted from the **React** framework, such as **Redux**, and **MobX**.

4
Adopting State Management Approaches from React

In the previous chapter, we learned about the most widely used state management approaches for Flutter apps and their slight variations. You can create almost all sorts of apps using what we have learned so far. But if you are coming from a React background, this chapter is for you.

This chapter focuses on two famous architectures that are adopted and inspired by the React framework. One of the techniques lets you manage your state in a single place inside your application, while the other one uses commands to autogenerate state management code so that you can solely focus on connecting your UI with your data. The following are these two techniques:

- **Redux** – One place for all states
- **MobX** – Observables and reactions

Let's understand what these two are and then dive into sample counterexamples of each of them.

Technical requirements

To successfully understand and execute everything explained in this chapter, you should have Flutter set up on your computer. Move over to Flutter's official website (`https://flutter.dev/docs/get-started/install`) and follow the steps based on your operating system.

If you already have Flutter set up on your computer, make sure your system's Flutter version is >=2. To check what the version of your previously installed Flutter is, go to Terminal (in macOS) or Command Prompt (in Windows) and run the following command:

```
flutter doctor
```

There are a number of IDEs that support Flutter. Some famous ones are VSCode, Android Studio, and IntelliJ IDEA. You can use any of them at your convenience.

The source code for this chapter is available in the following GitHub repository: `https://github.com/PacktPublishing/Managing-State-in-Flutter-Pragmatically/tree/main/ch4`.

Redux – using unidirectional data flow

Redux, in the simplest terms, is an architecture with a unidirectional data flow. This means the screens just call the actions out and the changes from Redux models are directed back to the screens through the stores.

Redux has four major keywords that you will have to understand before you move to the code:

- **Store** – Holds the state object of the whole application
- **Reducer** – Updates the state based on the action it receives
- **State** – The current snapshot of the application's UI
- **Actions** – The instructions to update the states

Let's look at all of them in code and see how they function together to create a state management solution.

Adding a Redux dependency to a sample app

Create a new app using any name you want, just like we did in the previous chapter:

```
flutter create any_name_you_wish
```

You will get the same counterexample application with the default `setState` implemented to update the counter value.

Let's see how to embed `Redux` into your application code:

1. Open up a browser and go to `https://pub.dev/`.

2. Type `redux` in the search bar and hit *Enter*.

3. Click on **flutter_redux**. It looks something like this:

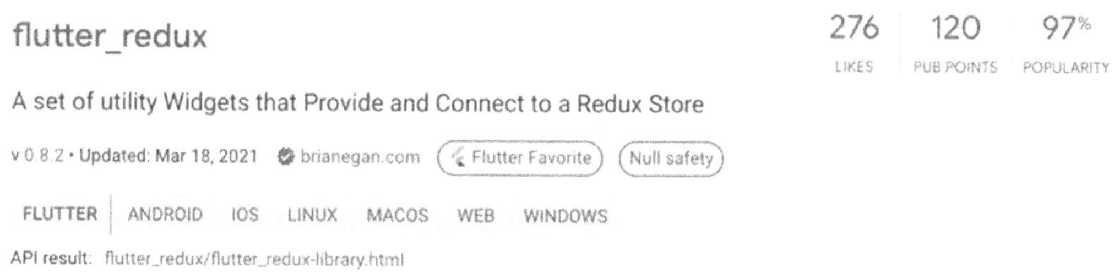

flutter_redux

276   120   97%
LIKES   PUB POINTS   POPULARITY

A set of utility Widgets that Provide and Connect to a Redux Store

v 0.8.2 · Updated: Mar 18, 2021   brianegan.com   (Flutter Favorite)   (Null safety)

FLUTTER | ANDROID   IOS   LINUX   MACOS   WEB   WINDOWS

API result: flutter_redux/flutter_redux-library.html

Figure 4.1 – The flutter_redux dependency on pub.dev

4. Once you are inside the **flutter_redux** package detail page, go to the **Installing** tab and copy the `flutter_redux: ^0.8.2` provider package dependency (the version may be different depending on the latest update).

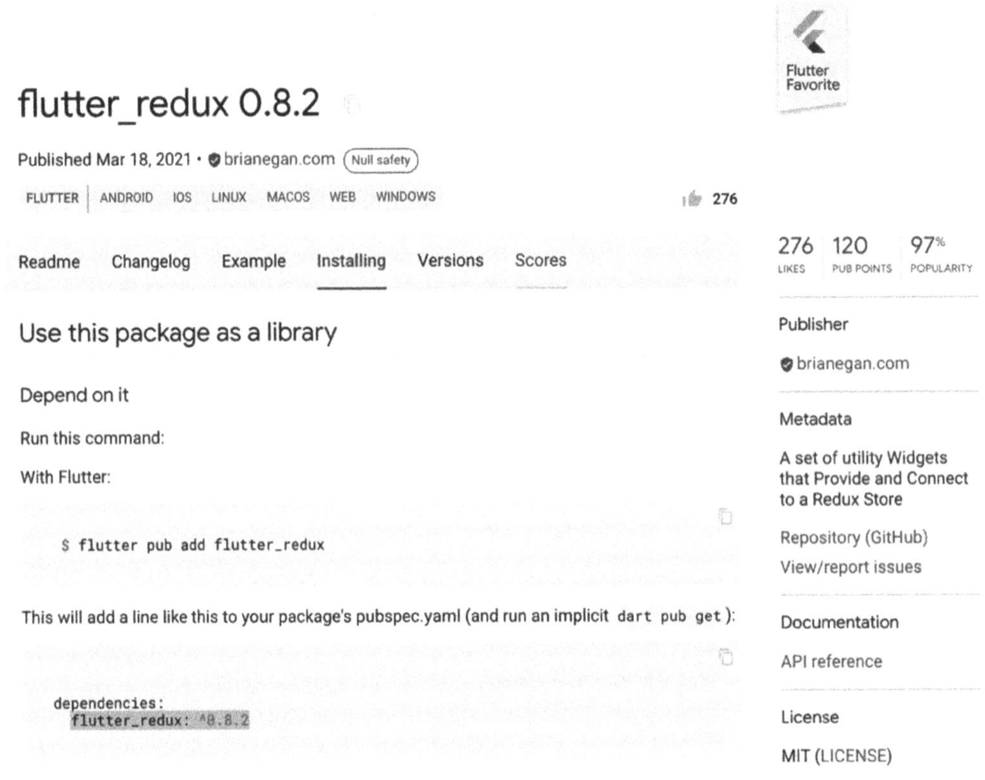
Flutter Favorite
flutter_redux 0.8.2
Published Mar 18, 2021 • brianegan.com Null safety
FLUTTER ANDROID IOS LINUX MACOS WEB WINDOWS
276
Readme Changelog Example Installing Versions Scores
276 LIKES 120 PUB POINTS 97% POPULARITY
Use this package as a library
Depend on it
Run this command:
With Flutter:
$ flutter pub add flutter_redux
This will add a line like this to your package's pubspec.yaml (and run an implicit dart pub get):
dependencies:
flutter_redux: ^0.8.2
Publisher
brianegan.com
Metadata
A set of utility Widgets that Provide and Connect to a Redux Store
Repository (GitHub)
View/report issues
Documentation
API reference
License
MIT (LICENSE)

Figure 4.2 – Dependency for flutter_redux

5. Go to your code and open the `pubspec.yaml` file present in your root folder.
6. Find the `dependencies` header and add the provider dependency under it:

```
dependencies:
  flutter:
    sdk: flutter
  flutter_redux: ^0.8.2
```

7. Make sure you keep the indents correct. The `flutter_redux` package declaration should be underneath the `flutter` declaration, as shown in the preceding code.

8. Your IDE should give a suggestion to run `flutter pub get` or `flutter packages get` in order to update the dependency that you just added. If not, you can open the terminal inside your IDE and type any of these two commands to update your dependency.

Now you are ready to consume the code of this package inside your app.

Consuming Redux using StoreProvider in code

We will be consuming the `flutter_redux` package in five brief steps:

1. Creating the `CounterState` class
2. Creating actions
3. Creating the `Reducer` function
4. Creating a global store
5. Consuming the store in our main UI

1. Creating the CounterState class

This is pretty simple. You just need to create a class with a constructor that represents your counter value inside the `main.dart` file in your `lib` directory:

```
class CounterState {
  final int count;

  CounterState({this.count = 0});
}
```

2. Creating actions

Actions can be of any type. They can be as simple as enums, or as complex as proper classes with properties. For our use case regarding the counterexample, we will use enums for now:

```
enum Actions { Increment, Decrement }
```

3. Creating the Reducer function

The `Reducer` function is declared globally, which handles all the events and updates the states accordingly:

```
CounterState counterReducer(CounterState state, dynamic action)
{
    if (action == Actions.Increment) {
      return CounterState(count: state.count + 1);
    }

    if (action == Actions.Decrement) {
      return CounterState(count: state.count - 1);
    }

    return state;
}
```

This function has a return type of `CounterState`, which will be used by our store.

4. Creating the store

The store is the heart of Redux state management. It stores the state, dispatches actions for `Reducer`, initializes the first state, and globally gives the state access to the whole app, all of this in a single line of code:

```
final store = Store<CounterState>(counterReducer, initialState:
CounterState());
```

It takes the type of our state (`CounterState`) as a type argument, our `Reducer` function as a parameter, and the initial state as a named parameter.

Let's combine all of this and make our UI functional.

5. Consuming the store in our main UI

We are going to wrap our application with `StoreProvider`. You should be very familiar with this. We have done this step in almost every advanced state management solution:

```
void main() {
    runApp(
```

```
    StoreProvider<CounterState>(
      store: store,
      child: MyApp(),
    ),
  );
}
```

In our main UI code, we will place a widget called `StoreConnector`, which takes the state and the data type of the variable you are going to use inside the connector, converts the state to that type, and allows you to put it inside your widget (in our case, that would be a `Text` widget):

```
Text('You have pushed this button this many times:',),
// New widget
StoreConnector<CounterState, String>(
  converter: (store) => store.state.count.toString(),
  builder: (context, count) {
    return Text(
      count,
      style: Theme.of(context).textTheme.headline4,
    );
  },
),
```

The new keyword here is the converter, which is returning the `count` variable as a string type in order for the builder to recognize it for the `Text` widget. This is similar to the `Consumer` widget we studied in the previous chapter, which listens to the changes done to the state.

Finally, we place our `dispatch` function inside the `onPressed` function of `FloatingActionButton`:

```
floatingActionButton: FloatingActionButton(
  onPressed: () => store.dispatch(Actions.Increment),
  child: Icon(Icons.add),
),
```

The `dispatch` function calls the `Reducer`, and the `Reducer` then decides which state to update based on the action that we pass as a parameter here.

Complete code in a single glance

Combining all of this, your UI code should look something like this if you keep it all in one single file:

```dart
import 'package:flutter/material.dart';
import 'package:flutter_redux/flutter_redux.dart';
import 'package:redux/redux.dart';

void main() {
  runApp(
    StoreProvider<CounterState>(
      store: store,
      child: MyApp(),
    ),
  );
}

class MyApp extends StatelessWidget {
  @override
  Widget build(BuildContext context) {
    return MaterialApp(
      title: 'Flutter Demo',
      theme: ThemeData(
        primarySwatch: Colors.blue,
      ),
      home: MyHomePage(title: 'Flutter Demo Home Page'),
    );
  }
}

class MyHomePage extends StatefulWidget {
  MyHomePage({Key? key, required this.title}) : super(key:
  key);
  final String title;

  @override
```

```
  _MyHomePageState createState() => _MyHomePageState();
}


class _MyHomePageState extends State<MyHomePage> {
  @override
  Widget build(BuildContext context) {
    return Scaffold(
      appBar: AppBar(
        title: Text(widget.title),
      ),
      body: Center(
        child: Column(
          mainAxisAlignment: MainAxisAlignment.center,
          children: <Widget>[
            Text(
              'You have pushed the button this many
              times:',
            ),
            StoreConnector<CounterState, String>(
              converter: (store) =>
              store.state.count.toString(),
              builder: (context, count) {
                return Text(
                  count,
                  style: Theme.of(context)
                  .textTheme.headline4,
                );
              },
            ),
          ],
        ),
      ),
      floatingActionButton: FloatingActionButton(
        onPressed: () => store.dispatch(Actions.Increment),
        child: Icon(Icons.add),
      ),
```

```dart
    );
  }
}

class CounterState {
  final int count;

  CounterState({this.count = 0});
}

enum Actions { Increment, Decrement }

CounterState counterReducer(CounterState state, dynamic action)
{
  if (action == Actions.Increment) {
    return CounterState(count: state.count + 1);
  }

  if (action == Actions.Decrement) {
    return CounterState(count: state.count - 1);
  }

  return state;
}

final store = Store<CounterState>(counterReducer, initialState:
CounterState());
```

Section overview – Redux

In this section, we learned the following:

- Redux is a unidirectional state management solution.
- flutter_redux is a Dart package that provides all the required functionality and keeps the boilerplate code inside itself.
- Redux uses a Reducer function to dispatch state changes based on the actions that it receives from the UI.

- The store is defined globally, which is used at all places throughout the application.
- `StoreConnector` is the widget that listens to the changes made by the `Reducer` function to the state.
- The `dispatch` function is used to trigger the `Reducer` function with an action that lets the `Reducer` function decide what state changes to perform.
- Actions can be of any type.

The next section is about MobX, which works on observables and reactions and lets you focus on consuming the data reactions in the UI without worrying about how they are being kept in sync.

MobX – using observables with the fewest lines of code

MobX is just another sort of reactive state management library that allows you to connect your reactive data directly to your UI using observables. The best part about MobX is that it requires the least amount of code you will need to create your apps. It takes away a lot of boilerplate code from you and allows you to generate most of it using the `build_runner` command.

We will study the following concepts in MobX:

- Observables
- Actions
- The `Observer` widget
- The Build runner dependency for the autogeneration of boilerplate code

Let's jump into setting up dependencies to create our counterexample application.

Adding MobX, Build Runner, and Codegen dependencies to the sample app

Just like on every other occasion, create a new Flutter app through the command line:

```
flutter create any_name_you_wish
```

You will get the same counterexample application with a default `setState` widget implemented to update the counter value. Rename your `MyHomePage` class to `CounterMobxExample`.

In Mobx, we will be integrating more than one library in our app for the whole setup to work. We will be using the mobx, flutter_mobx, build_runner, and mobx_codegen libraries from pub.dev. Since you have been following this step in every section, you might not want to go through the whole process again:

1. Open up a browser and go to https://pub.dev/.

2. Type each of the libraries mentioned previously and pick their latest dependency from their websites' **Installing** tabs.

3. The only difference in mentioning these libraries is that you have to put mobx and flutter_mobx under the dependencies tag in your pubspec.yaml file, whereas the build_runner and mobx_codegen dependencies will go under the dev_dependencies tag. It should look something like this after you have integrated all the dependencies:

```
dependencies:
  flutter:
    sdk: flutter
  flutter_mobx: ^2.0.0
  mobx: ^2.0.1

dev_dependencies:
  flutter_test:
    sdk: flutter
  build_runner: ^2.0.4
  mobx_codegen: ^2.0.1+3
```

4. Your IDE should suggest running flutter pub get or flutter packages get to update the dependency that you just added. If not, you can open the terminal inside your IDE and type any of these two commands to update your dependency.

Let's use flutter_mobx in our example application to convert our counterexample from setState to mobx.

Using code generation to create boilerplate code through build runner

Creating a counterexample app is simple in MobX. Let's create one with these simple steps:

1. Create your `Counter` class in a new file named `counter.dart` inside the `lib` directory. This will actually be an abstract class and its implementation will be autogenerated:

    ```
    import 'package:mobx/mobx.dart';


    part 'counter.g.dart';


    class Counter = _Counter with _$Counter;


    abstract class _Counter with Store {
      @observable
      int value = 0;


      @action
      void increment() {
        value++;
      }
    }
    ```

    There are two overridden keywords, `observable` and `action`, which come from the `Store` mixin declared inside the `mobx` dependency. When you create this file, you will get an error on `counter.g.dart` because this file doesn't exist yet. Let's create this file using a command.

2. Go to Terminal/CMD and type the following inside your root folder for the project:

    `flutter packages pub run build_runner build`

    This is going to create a `counter.g.dart` file with your `counter` class. This file has all the boilerplate code that you don't want to worry about and must not change.

3. Next, you will create an instance of your `Counter` class inside your `State` class in the `main.dart` file:

```
class MyHomePageState extends State<MyHomePage> {
   final Counter counter = Counter();
... ...
```

4. Create the `Observer` widget and wrap your `Text` widget around it:

```
Observer(
   builder: (_) => Text(
     '${counter.value}',
     style: const TextStyle(fontSize: 40),
   ),
 ),
```

This is similar to `Consumer` in Provider and `StoreConnector` in Redux. This is going to listen to the changes made to your counter variable and update the UI automatically.

5. The final step is, as usual, to put the `increment` action on our `FloatingActionButton` button:

```
floatingActionButton: FloatingActionButton(
   onPressed: counter.increment,
   child: const Icon(Icons.add),
 ),
```

You can now run your code, and if you have followed all the steps correctly, it should work as expected. You can add more actions to your `Counter` class.

> **Note**
>
> Make sure to run the build runner command after every time you make changes to your `Counter` class. You will have to regenerate the `counter.g.dart` file again to reflect the changes.

MobX – section overview

In this section, we understood some basic notions about the MobX state management library. The library has the least boilerplate code of all. This allows us to focus on creating better flows by autogenerating major state management code through the build runner command. We learned how multiple dependencies and `dev_dependencies` combine to create the seamless integration of the UI with the data.

Summary

We learned about two approaches from React in this chapter: Redux and MobX. Both of the approaches used reactive-style programming where you create actions and listen through observables. To summarize, we have the following:

- Redux uses a unidirectional data flow to manage the state in your Flutter app.

- Redux uses a single store that keeps the whole state of your application.

- MobX uses the autogeneration of state management code, hence it is easier to understand and implement.

- The `build_runner` command generates the part of the file that is connected to the class created by us.

The two React-adopted techniques we learned about in this chapter are going to be helpful to you if you are coming from a React background and have used Redux in your React projects very often. Also, if you want to experience how autogeneration is helpful in large-scale apps, MobX is going to be your go-to technique.

In the next chapter, we will be studying some distinctive state management approaches, such as **GetX**, **GetIt**, and **Binder**, which are created to make certain use cases easier.

5

Executing Distinctive Approaches Like GetX, GetIt, and Binder

In the previous chapter, we studied state management approaches adopted from the **React** framework, which included **Redux** and **MobX**.

In this chapter, we will discuss some distinctive state management approaches that are relatively simpler, easier, and require less understanding of the underlying architecture. We will learn about **GetX**, **GetIt**, and **Binder** to manage states in **Flutter**. We will also look at how these approaches are utilized in code with actual implementations. We will look into the following in this chapter:

- GetX – simplified reactive approach
- GetIt – no `BuildContext` required
- Binder – separation of concerns

This chapter is going to build up your understanding of how these distinctive approaches can be used to detect and track the changes inside a Flutter application. By the end of this chapter, you should be able to do the following:

- Understand how to implement a basic page with a single-button user interaction and manage its state using all three of the state management approaches described.

- Differentiate between these three state management approaches.

Technical requirements

In order to successfully understand and execute everything explained in this chapter, you should have Flutter set up on your computer:

`https://flutter.dev/docs/get-started/install`

If you already have Flutter set up, make sure your version is at least *version 2*. To check your current version, go to **Terminal** (in **macOS**) or **Command Prompt** (in **Windows**) and run the following command:

```
flutter doctor
```

You can use any **IDE** that supports Flutter. Some well-known ones are **VSCode**, **Android Studio**, and **IntelliJ IDEA**.

All the code shown in this chapter is uploaded (in complete form) on **GitHub**: `https://github.com/PacktPublishing/Managing-State-in-Flutter-Pragmatically/tree/main/ch5`.

GetX – simplified reactions

GetX is one of the simplest state management techniques that uses the least possible boilerplate code to manage your states in Flutter. It abstracts out all the repetitive code for you and lets you write your main code with the smallest number of lines. GetX is also known for abstracting out navigation logic and providing a clean interface for handling navigations in your application. To deeply understand the theory and motivation behind GetX, read the documentation on their official package ReadMe page:

```
https://pub.dev/packages/get
```

Let's see how our counter example is built using GetX.

Adding a GetX dependency in a sample application

Create a new application using any name you want just like we did in the previous chapters:

```
flutter create any_name_you_wish
```

You will get the same counter example application with the default `setState` management technique implemented to update the counter value.

Let's see how to embed GetX into your application code:

1. Open up a browser and go to `https://pub.dev/`.

2. Type `getX` in the search bar and hit *Enter*.

3. Click on **get**. It looks something like this:

get   5354   120   99%
                                                     LIKES   PUB POINTS POPULARITY

Open screens/snackbars/dialogs without context, manage states and inject dependencies easily with GetX.

v 4.1.4 · Updated. Apr 11, 2021   🌐 getx.site   (Null safety)

FLUTTER | ANDROID   IOS   LINUX   MACOS   WEB   WINDOWS

Figure 5.1 – The GetX dependency on pub.dev

4. Once you are on the `get` package detail page, go to the **Installing** tab and copy the provider package dependency, `get: ^4.1.4` (the version may be different depending on the latest update).

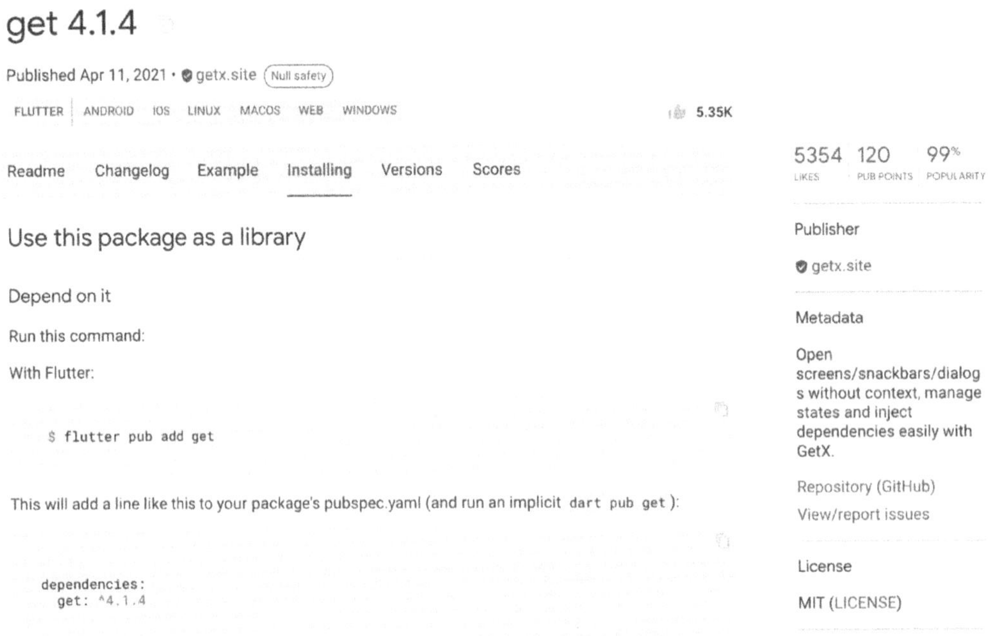

get 4.1.4

Published Apr 11, 2021 • ✅ getx.site   (Null safety)

FLUTTER | ANDROID IOS LINUX MACOS WEB WINDOWS   👍 **5.35K**

5354	**120**	**99%**
LIKES	PUB POINTS	POPULARITY

Readme   Changelog   Example   Installing   Versions   Scores

Use this package as a library

Depend on it

Run this command:

With Flutter:

```
$ flutter pub add get
```

This will add a line like this to your package's pubspec.yaml (and run an implicit `dart pub get`):

```
dependencies:
    get: ^4.1.4
```

Publisher

✅ getx.site

Metadata

Open screens/snackbars/dialogs without context, manage states and inject dependencies easily with GetX.

Repository (GitHub)
View/report issues

License

MIT (LICENSE)

Figure 5.2 – Dependency for GetX

5. Go to your code and open the `pubspec.yaml` file present in your root folder.

6. Find the `dependencies` header and add the `get` dependency under it:

```
dependencies:
  flutter:
    sdk: flutter
  get: ^4.1.4
```

7. Make sure you add the indents correctly. The `get` package declaration should be underneath the `flutter` declaration, as shown in the preceding code example.

8. Your IDE should give a suggestion to run `flutter pub get` or `flutter packages get` in order to update the dependency that you just added. If not, you can open the terminal inside your IDE and type any of these two commands to update your dependency.

Now, you are ready to consume the code of this package inside your application.

Example of a counter application using GetBuilder

There are basically three ways you can use `Get` packages, inside your UI, to manage states in your application:

- `GetxController` – Reactive programming, which includes listeners and a stream-like structure to update changes in the UI

- `GetBuilder` – Simple, clean state management

- `Obs` – Syntax friendly

There can be multiple ways to use the preceding three methods. We will be using them in combination with implementing the `GetBuilder` widget in our example due to its enriched feasibility and the fact that we will use the same technique in the upcoming chapters. This means we will be using the `GetBuilder` widget in our UI to listen to the changes done by the package. This does not mean we won't be using the other two keywords at all. You can read more about all the approaches in the `ReadMe` section of the package.

In the following example, you will come across the following new code-level keywords:

- `GetMaterialApp` – The root widget of your application that replaces the `MaterialApp` widget

- `GetxController` – The controller class (similar to the previous state management approaches we studied, the `State` class with the `reducer` function in *Redux* and the abstract `Counter` class implementing `Store` in *MobX*)

- `GetBuilder` – The widget that wraps the actual UI in order to show the updated changes in the variables

- `.obs` – The keyword to convert any variable or class into an `observable` object

Let's begin with our counter example application:

1. First, inside the `main.dart` file, delete the `MyHomePage` class.

2. Then, rename `_MyHomePageState` as `MyHomePage`.

3. Next, make your new `MyHomePage` class extend from `StatelessWidget` and update `MaterialApp` to `GetMaterialApp` inside the `MyApp` class. Your `MyApp` class should look something like this:

```
class MyApp extends StatelessWidget {
  @override
  Widget build(BuildContext context) {
    return GetMaterialApp(          // updated
```

```
      title: 'Flutter Demo',
      theme: ThemeData(
        primarySwatch: Colors.blue,
      ),
      home: MyHomePage(),
    );
  }
}
```

This `GetMaterialApp` widget enables all the state management boilerplate code for you, which will allow you to directly manage variables' states with minimum code.

4. Now, create a simple `Counter` class:

```
class Counter {
  int count;

  Counter({required this.count});
}
```

5. Next, create a controller class that will manage this `Counter` class:

```
class CounterController extends GetxController {
  var counter = (Counter(count: 0)).obs;

  void increment() {
    counter.value.count++;
    update();
  }
}
```

Make sure to add the `import` statement:

```
Import 'package:get/get.dart';
```

The `GetxController` class allows you to use abstracted boilerplate code and extend observable functionalities from the `Get` package. The `.obs` keyword allows you to make a variable observable so that, whenever it changes, the UI should know. The update function acts like a `setState` function here.

6. In the UI code, inside the `MyHomePage` class, you simply need to wrap your `Text` widget with a `GetBuilder` widget:

```
GetBuilder(
  builder: (CounterController controller) {
    return Text(
      controller.counter.value.count.toString(),
      style: Theme.of(context).textTheme.headline4,
    );
  },
),
```

This `GetBuilder` widget rebuilds itself whenever there is any change done to the `CounterController` properties.

7. Also, the preceding code will give you an error on `controller` because this is something that doesn't exist right now. So, we add the following line inside the `build` method of your class:

```
class MyHomePage extends StatelessWidget {
  @override
  Widget build(BuildContext context) {
    CounterController controller =
    Get.put(CounterController()); // new code
  ... ...
```

`Get.put` is quite self-explanatory. This function puts the instance of your controller class in the tree. This gives you the privilege to leverage your controller class's state anywhere and on any page in your application just by using the following line:

```
CounterController controller = Get.find();
```

This will automatically find the instance of the `CounterController` type that was previously kept in the tree using the `Get.put` function.

Collectively, your complete file should look like this:

```
import 'package:flutter/material.dart';
import 'package:get/get.dart';

void main() {
  runApp(MyApp());
}

class Counter {
  int count;

  Counter({required this.count});
}

class CounterController extends GetxController {
  var counter = (Counter(count: 0)).obs;

  void increment() {
    counter.value.count++;
    update();
  }
}

class MyApp extends StatelessWidget {
  @override
  Widget build(BuildContext context) {
    return GetMaterialApp(
      title: 'Flutter Demo',
      theme: ThemeData(
        primarySwatch: Colors.blue,
      ),
      home: MyHomePage(),
    );
  }
```

```
}

class MyHomePage extends StatelessWidget {
  @override
  Widget build(BuildContext context) {
    CounterController controller =
    Get.put(CounterController());
    return Scaffold(
      appBar: AppBar(
        title: Text('GetX example'),
      ),
      body: Center(
        child: Column(
          mainAxisAlignment: MainAxisAlignment.center,
          children: <Widget>[
            Text(
              'You have pushed the button this many
              times:',
            ),
            GetBuilder(
              builder: (CounterController controller) {
                return Text(
                  controller.counter.value.
                  count.toString(),
                  style: Theme.of(context)
                  .textTheme.headline4,
                );
              },
            ),
          ],
        ),
      ),
      floatingActionButton: FloatingActionButton(
        onPressed: () => controller.increment(),
```

```
        child: Icon(Icons.add),
      ),
    );
  }
}
```

Here is the expected end result:

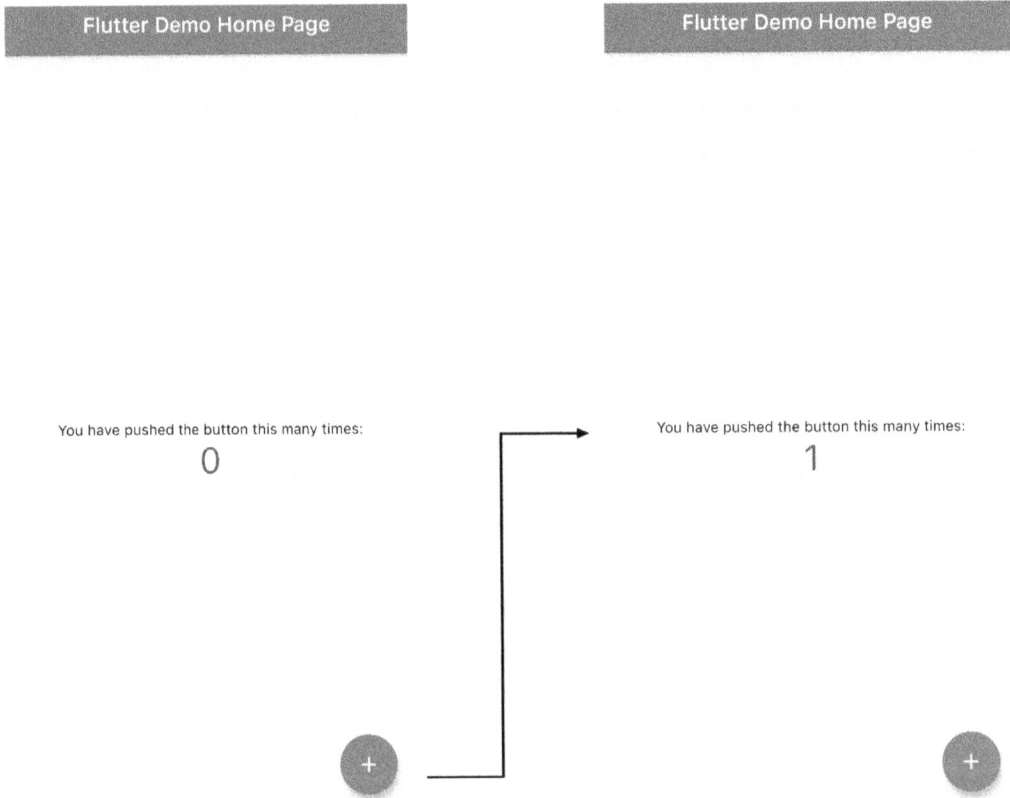

Figure 5.3 – The expected end result

Exploring more in GetX

GetX is not only restricted to state management. It also simplifies navigation systems as well. Our normal navigation code looks something like this:

```
Navigator.of(context).push(
  MaterialPageRoute(
```

```
    builder: (context) => MyNewPage(),
  ),
);
```

But, with GetX, it is going to be much shorter and simpler:

```
Get.to(MyNewPage());
```

This makes it easier to write more logic in fewer lines of code and provides better code readability. GetX also makes dependency management, HTTP calls, theme management, internationalization, and more simpler and more feasible. You can read more about these at the official library page (`https://pub.dev/packages/get`).

Section overview – GetX

In this section, we learned the following:

- How to use GetX to create a counter example application.
- How to use the `GetBuilder` widget to wrap the `Text` widget.
- How the `GetMaterialApp` widget abstracts out all the boilerplate code for us.
- GetX is not only restricted to state management.
- How it is simpler to create navigation code using GetX.

Let's look at a nice challenge that will get your hands dirty with GetX.

Optional challenge – GetX

Before we move on to the next section, here is a little optional challenge for your brain. You are to create three screens:

- Main page
- Screen A
- Screen B

The main page should have a `Text` widget showing the counter value (with the default set to 1) and two buttons. Each of the buttons navigates to screen A and screen B respectively. Screens A and B both have a `Text` widget showing the counter they receive from the main page and a button for incrementing the counter.

Now for the challenge. Both screens A and B should be able to update the counter, and the latest updated counter value should be seen in all three screens.

> **Note**
>
> You are not allowed to send the counter variable in page constructors.

The next section discusses GetIt. This is a technique that uses dependency injection to inject model classes, instances of which can be used within the whole application. Under the hood, this technique uses functionality similar to `setState`.

GetIt – no BuildContext required

GetIt is an approach that uses the `setState` functionality to update the UI and leverages the power of dependency injection to give access to model classes to the whole application. It also doesn't require `BuildContext` to update and manage any states anywhere inside your application.

> **Note**
>
> If you want to learn more about dependency injection in general, please visit the wiki page (`https://en.wikipedia.org/wiki/Dependency_injection`).

Let's see how our counter example is built using GetIt.

Adding a GetIt dependency in a sample application

Create a new application using any name you want, just like we did in the previous chapters:

```
flutter create any_name_you_wish
```

You will get the same counter example application with the default `setState` management technique implemented to update the counter value.

Let's see how to embed GetIt into your application code:

1.   Open up a browser and go to `https://pub.dev/`.

2.   Type `getIt` in the search bar and hit *Enter*.

3.   Click on **get_it**. It looks something like this:

get_it

1357 130 99%
LIKES PUB POINTS POPULARITY

Simple direct Service Locator that allows to decouple the interface from a concrete implementation and to access the concrete implementation from everywhere in your App"

v 7.2.0 · Updated: Jul 13, 2021   ● fluttercommunity.dev   (Null safety)

DART | NATIVE JS | FLUTTER | ANDROID IOS LINUX MACOS WEB WINDOWS

API result: get_it/GetIt-class.html

Figure 5.4 – The GetIt dependency on pub.dev

4. Once you are on the `get_it` package detail page, go to the **Installing** tab and copy the provider package dependency, `get_it: ^7.2.0` (the version may be different depending on the latest update).

get_it 7.2.0

Published Jul 13, 2021 · ● fluttercommunity.dev (Null safety)

DART | NATIVE JS | FLUTTER | ANDROID IOS LINUX MACOS WEB WINDOWS   1.36K

Readme   Changelog   Example   Installing   Versions   Scores

Use this package as a library

Depend on it

Run this command:

With Dart:

```
$ dart pub add get_it
```

With Flutter:

```
$ flutter pub add get_it
```

This will add a line like this to your package's pubspec.yaml (and run an implicit `dart pub get`):

```
dependencies:
  get_it: ^7.2.0
```

1357 130 99%
LIKES PUB POINTS POPULARITY

Publisher

● fluttercommunity.dev

Metadata

Simple direct Service Locator that allows to decouple the interface from a concrete implementation and to access the concrete implementation from everywhere in your App"

Repository (GitHub)
View/report issues

Documentation

API reference

License

MIT (LICENSE)

Figure 5.5 – Dependency for GetIt

5. Go to your code and open the `pubspec.yaml` file present in your root folder.

6. Find the `dependencies` header and add the `get_it` dependency under it:

```
dependencies:
  flutter:
    sdk: flutter
  get_it: ^7.2.0
```

7. Make sure you add the indents correctly. The `get_it` package declaration should be underneath the `flutter` declaration, as shown in the preceding code example.

8. Your IDE should give a suggestion to run `flutter pub get` or `flutter packages get` in order to update the dependency that you just added. If not, you can open the terminal inside your IDE and type any of these two commands to update your dependency.

Now, you are ready to consume the code of this package inside your application.

Counter example application using GetIt

Just like in every other approach, the first step would be to create a counter model class that will keep our state variable. So, let's begin:

1. Create a **Dart** file named `counter_model.dart` and add the following code:

```dart
import 'package:flutter/material.dart';

class CounterModel extends ChangeNotifier {
  int _counter = 0;

  int get counter => _counter;

  void incrementCounter() {
    _counter++;
    notifyListeners();
  }
}
```

Note, this class is very similar to something we created in *Chapter 2, The Core Building Blocks of State Management* (in the *Provider* section). This class is extended by a `ChangeNotifier` class, which means that this class will be listened to by the UI for changes. Similarly, we have the `notifyListeners()` function, which gets triggered every time the increment function is called.

2. Now, let's move into our `main.dart` file and add a GetIt global instance and the `CounterModel` initialization. Update your main function with the register function, and add a global `GetIt` variable:

```
import 'package:flutter/material.dart';
// new import
import 'package:get_it/get_it.dart';


import 'counter_model.dart';


GetIt = GetIt.instance;


void main() {
  // new code
  getIt.registerSingleton<CounterModel>
  (CounterModel(), signalsReady: true);


  runApp(MyApp());
}
... ... ...
```

The `registerSingleton` function does exactly what it's named after. It registers a single instance of our `CounterModel` class, which will be used by the whole application using dependency injection.

The `signalsReady` Bool is for letting the code know when the singleton class is ready to return a future. This is related to the next step, which is adding a constructor to our `CounterModel` class:

```
import 'package:flutter/material.dart';


// new import
import 'main.dart';
```

```
class CounterModel extends ChangeNotifier {
  int _counter = 0;

  int get counter => _counter;

// new code
  CounterModel() {
    Future.delayed(Duration(milliseconds:
    100)).then((_) => getIt.signalReady(this));
  }
//

  void incrementCounter() {
    _counter++;
    notifyListeners();
  }
}
```

This `signalReady` function tells GetIt that it's now ready to be used. A delay is added so that the UI builds before this class is built.

3. Let's consume all of this setup in our UI class. Add the following code in your home page state class:

```
@override
void initState() {
  getIt.isReady<CounterModel>().then((_) =>
  getIt<CounterModel>().addListener(update));
  // Alternative
  // getIt.getAsync<CounterModel>()
    .addListener(update);

  super.initState();
}

@override
void dispose() {
  getIt<CounterModel>().removeListener(update);
```

```
    super.dispose();
  }
```

```
  void update() => setState(() => {});
```

In the `initState` function, you need to call the `isReady` function on the `CounterModel` class and add a `setState` function to its listener. This will enable the updates to the UI whenever the increment function is called from the `CounterModel` class. In `dispose`, we remove that listener.

The `build` method of your home page state class should look something like this:

```
@override
Widget build(BuildContext context) {
  return Material(
    // One
    child: FutureBuilder(
        future: getIt.allReady(),
        builder: (context, snapshot) {
          if (snapshot.hasData) {
            return Scaffold(
              appBar: AppBar(
                title: Text(widget.title),
              ),
              body: Center(
                child: Column(
                  mainAxisAlignment:
                  MainAxisAlignment.center,
                  children: <Widget>[
                    Text(
                      'You have pushed the button this many
                      times:',
                    ),
                    // Two
                    Text(
                    getIt<CounterModel>()
                    .counter.toString(),
                      style: Theme.of(context)
```

```
                  .textTheme.headline4,
              ),
          ],
        ),
      ),
// Three
      floatingActionButton: FloatingActionButton(
        onPressed: getIt<CounterModel>()
        .incrementCounter,
        tooltip: 'Increment',
        child: Icon(Icons.add),
      ),
    );
  } else {
// Four
    return Column(
      mainAxisAlignment: MainAxisAlignment.center,
      mainAxisSize: MainAxisSize.min,
      children: [
        Text('Waiting for initialisation'),
        SizedBox(
          height: 16,
        ),
        CircularProgressIndicator(),
      ],
    );
  }
})),
  );
}
```

This creates your overall page for the counter application using GetIt. There are highlighted comments in the code block that are explained in order as follows:

- One: This is a simple `FutureBuilder` widget that takes `getIt.allReady` as its parameter. The `allReady` function returns a future whenever the `CounterModel` class has completed its initialization. Underneath `future` is the `builder` parameter, which returns widgets depending on the current state of the snapshot returned by the future.

- Two: Using dependency injection, we get the latest counter variable value from our singleton `CounterModel` class.

- Three: Similarly, we call the `incrementCounter` function, which is declared inside our singleton `CounterModel` class.

- Four: Until all the singletons are ready (in our case, it's only `CounterModel`), the UI will be waiting for initialization.

Now, your completed main class should look something like this:

```
import 'package:flutter/material.dart';
import 'package:get_it/get_it.dart';


import 'counter_model.dart';


GetIt = GetIt.instance;

void main() {
  getIt.registerSingleton<CounterModel>(CounterModel(),
  signalsReady: true);


  runApp(MyApp());
}


class MyApp extends StatelessWidget {
  // This widget is the root of your application.
  @override
  Widget build(BuildContext context) {
    return MaterialApp(
      title: 'Flutter Demo',
      theme: ThemeData(
```

```dart
        primarySwatch: Colors.blue,
      ),
      home: MyHomePage(title: 'Flutter Demo Home Page'),
    );
  }
}

class MyHomePage extends StatefulWidget {
  MyHomePage({Key? key, required this.title}) : super(key:
  key);

  final String title;

  @override
  _MyHomePageState createState() => _MyHomePageState();
}

class _MyHomePageState extends State<MyHomePage> {
  @override
  void initState() {
    getIt.isReady<CounterModel>().then((_) =>
    getIt<CounterModel>().addListener(update));
    // Alternative
    // getIt.getAsync<CounterModel>().addListener(update);

    super.initState();
  }

  @override
  void dispose() {
    getIt<CounterModel>().removeListener(update);
    super.dispose();
  }

  void update() => setState(() => {});
```

```
@override
Widget build(BuildContext context) {
  return Material(
    child: FutureBuilder(
        future: getIt.allReady(),
        builder: (context, snapshot) {
          if (snapshot.hasData) {
            return Scaffold(
              appBar: AppBar(
                title: Text(widget.title),
              ),
              body: Center(
                child: Column(
                  mainAxisAlignment:
                  MainAxisAlignment.center,
                  children: <Widget>[
                    Text(
                      'You have pushed the button this
                        many times:',
                    ),
                    Text(
                      getIt<CounterModel>()
                      .counter.toString(),
                      style: Theme.of(context)
                      .textTheme.headline4,
                    ),
                  ],
                ),
              ),
              floatingActionButton: FloatingActionButton(
                onPressed: getIt<CounterModel>()
                .incrementCounter,
                tooltip: 'Increment',
                child: Icon(Icons.add),
              ),
            );
```

```
      } else {
        return Column(
          mainAxisAlignment:
          MainAxisAlignment.center,
          mainAxisSize: MainAxisSize.min,
          children: [
            Text('Waiting for initialisation'),
            SizedBox(
              height: 16,
            ),
            CircularProgressIndicator(),
          ],
        );
      }
    }),
  );
}
}
```

Section overview – GetIt

In this brief section, we learned the following about GetIt:

- It uses dependency injection and `setState` to manage states.
- It creates singleton instances of all the models that we intend to use in our application.
- It has a global instance declared at the top of the application.

The next section is about Binder. This is a state management technique that binds the UI to the business logic using *scopes*.

Binder – using scopes to separate business logic

Binder, just like any popular state management solution, aims to separate business logic from the main UI code, which makes it easier to manage, read, test, and update the code. Binder uses states and scopes to manage and separate business logic from the UI. Let's add the package dependency for Binder and create our counter example application.

Adding a Binder dependency in a sample application

Create a new application using any name you want, just like we did in the previous chapters:

```
flutter create any_name_you_wish
```

You will get the same counter example application with the default `setState` management technique implemented to update the counter value.

Let's see how to embed Binder into your application code:

1. Open up a browser and go to `https://pub.dev/`.
2. Type `binder` in the search bar and hit *Enter*.
3. Click on **binder**. It looks something like this:

binder

| 42 | 120 | 62% |
| LIKES | PUB POINTS | POPULARITY |

A lightweight, yet powerful way to bind your application state with your business logic.

v 0.4.0 · Updated: Mar 25, 2021   ✔ romainrastel.com   (Null safety)

FLUTTER | ANDROID   IOS   LINUX   MACOS   WEB   WINDOWS

Figure 5.6- The Binder dependency on pub.dev

4. Once you are on the `binder` package detail page, go to the **Installing** tab and copy the provider package dependency, `binder: ^0.4.0` (the version may be different depending on the latest update).

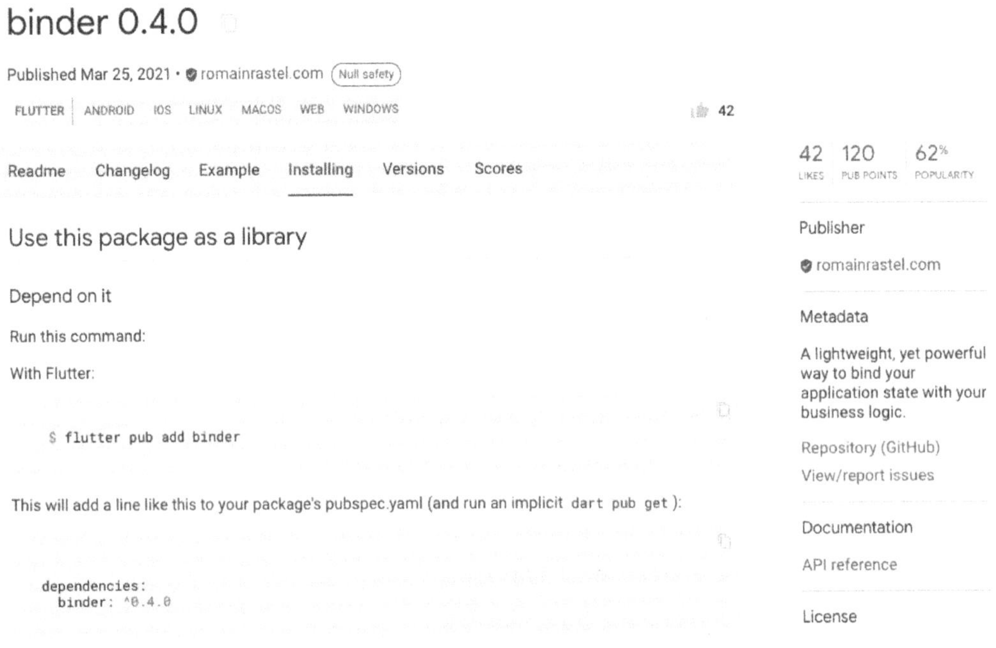

binder 0.4.0

Published Mar 25, 2021 • 🛡 romainrastel.com (Null safety)

FLUTTER | ANDROID   IOS   LINUX   MACOS   WEB   WINDOWS   👍 42

Readme   Changelog   Example   Installing   Versions   Scores

---

Use this package as a library

Depend on it

Run this command:

With Flutter:

```
$ flutter pub add binder
```

This will add a line like this to your package's pubspec.yaml (and run an implicit `dart pub get`):

```
dependencies:
  binder: ^0.4.0
```

	42	120	62%
	LIKES	PUB POINTS	POPULARITY

Publisher

🛡 romainrastel.com

Metadata

A lightweight, yet powerful way to bind your application state with your business logic.

Repository (GitHub)

View/report issues

Documentation

API reference

License

Figure 5.7 – Dependency for Binder

5. Go to your code and open the `pubspec.yaml` file present in your root folder.

6. Find the `dependencies` header and add the `binder` dependency under it:

```
dependencies:
  flutter:
    sdk: flutter
  binder: ^0.4.0
```

7. Make sure you add the indents correctly. The `binder` package declaration should be underneath the `flutter` declaration, as shown in the preceding code example.

8. Your IDE should give a suggestion to run `flutter pub get` or `flutter packages get` in order to update the dependency that you just added. If not, you can open the terminal inside your IDE and type any of these two commands to update your dependency.

Now, you are ready to consume the code of this package inside your application.

Counter example application using Binder

Like every other approach, the first step would be to create a counter model class. Create a new Dart file named counter_model.dart and add a CounterModel class:

```
class CounterModel {
  int count;

  CounterModel({required this.count});
}
```

There are three major steps that we will perform before we move on to our main UI code:

1. Create a global state variable using a StateRef object. Add the following line to your counter_model.dart file outside of the CounterModel class:

    ```
    Import 'package:binder/binder.dart';
    final counterRef = StateRef(CounterModel(count: 0));
    ```

    This is how you declare a state variable in Binder. The StateRef object takes your initial class instance as a parameter and initializes a global state with a default counter value of zero. This counterRef variable will be used in our main UI code to read the latest counter value.

2. Next, we will add a view logic class that will be responsible for separating the UI from our logic. Add the following code in the counter_model.dart file:

    ```
    class CounterViewLogic with Logic {
      const CounterViewLogic(this.scope);

      @override
      final Scope; // Binder scope

      void increment() {
        var counter = CounterModel(count:
        ++read(counterRef).count);
        write(counterRef, counter);
      }
    }
    ```

The `CounterViewLogic` class uses the `Logic` mixin inside the `Binder` package for using the overridden scope variable. This scope is passed as a parameter when we declare our global logic variable, which takes us to the next step.

3. Add the following code as a global variable in your `counter_model.dart` file:

```
final counterViewLogicRef = LogicRef((scope) =>
CounterViewLogic(scope));
```

This is how we declare logic in Binder. The `LogicRef` class provides you with a scope every time you create a new object, which is passed to our `CounterViewLogic` class. This `counterViewLogicRef` will be used inside our main UI to increment the counter.

Now, let's move on to our main UI code in order to connect all the previous code that we wrote:

1. The first step is to wrap `MaterialApp` in the `BinderScope` widget in order to enable all the boilerplate code that is embedded in the `Binder` package. Update your `MyApp` class to add a `Binder` widget around your `MaterialApp` widget:

```
class MyApp extends StatelessWidget {
  @override
  Widget build(BuildContext context) {
    return BinderScope( // new code
      child: MaterialApp(
        title: 'Flutter Demo',
        theme: ThemeData(
          primarySwatch: Colors.blue,
        ),
        home: MyHomePage(),
      ),
    );
  }
}
```

Don't forget to add the Binder dependency import at the top:

```
import 'package:binder/binder.dart';
```

2. Next, delete the `MyHomePage` class.

3. Then, rename `_MyHomePageState` as `MyHomePage`.

4. Next, make your new MyHomePage class extend StatelessWidget, remove the _incrementCounter function and the _counter variable, and add the following code inside the build method:

```
final counter = context.watch(counterRef);
```

This will enable you to read the latest value of your CounterModel class. You will have to add the counter_model.dart import at the top:

```
import 'counter_model.dart';
```

5. Update your Text widget to use the preceding counter variable:

```
Text(
  counter.count.toString(),
  style: Theme.of(context).textTheme.headline4,
)
```

6. Update the onPressed property of your FloatingActionButton widget to use the counterViewLogicRef variable declared earlier:

```
floatingActionButton: FloatingActionButton(
  onPressed: () => context.use(counterViewLogicRef)
  .increment(),
  tooltip: 'Increment',
  child: const Icon(Icons.add),
),
```

And we are done! Your main UI file should look something like this:

```
import 'package:flutter/material.dart';
import 'package:binder/binder.dart';

import 'counter_model.dart';

void main() {
  runApp(MyApp());
}

class MyApp extends StatelessWidget {
  @override
```

```dart
Widget build(BuildContext context) {
  return BinderScope(
    child: MaterialApp(
      title: 'Flutter Demo',
      theme: ThemeData(
        primarySwatch: Colors.blue,
      ),
      home: MyHomePage(),
    ),
  );
}
}

class MyHomePage extends StatelessWidget {
  @override
  Widget build(BuildContext context) {
    final counter = context.watch(counterRef);
    return Scaffold(
      appBar: AppBar(title: const Text('Binder example')),
      body: Center(
        child: Column(
          mainAxisAlignment: MainAxisAlignment.center,
          children: <Widget>[
            const Text('You have pushed the button this
            many times:'),
            Text(
              counter.count.toString(),
              style: Theme.of(context).textTheme.headline4,
            ),
          ],
        ),
      ),
      floatingActionButton: FloatingActionButton(
        onPressed: () => context.use(counterViewLogicRef)
        .increment(),
        tooltip: 'Increment',
```

```
            child: const Icon(Icons.add),
          ),
        );
      }
    }
```

Your `counter_model.dart` file should look something like this, with all the state and logic reference variables combined:

```dart
import 'package:binder/binder.dart';

class CounterModel {
  int count;

  CounterModel({required this.count});
}

final counterRef = StateRef(CounterModel(count: 0));

final counterViewLogicRef = LogicRef((scope) =>
CounterViewLogic(scope));

class CounterViewLogic with Logic {
  const CounterViewLogic(this.scope);

  @override
  final Scope;

  void increment() {
    var counter = CounterModel(count:
    ++read(counterRef).count);
    write(counterRef, counter);
  }
}
```

Now, you can run your code and check to see whether your counter value updates itself.

Section overview – Binder

In this brief section, we learned the following about Binder:

- It uses scopes and `StateRef` to manage states.
- It uses a `Logic` mixin to decouple the UI from the business logic.
- It creates global variables of both state references and views logic classes.
- The `BinderScope` widget is wrapped around the `MaterialApp` widget in order to enable all the boilerplate code from the `Binder` package.

Summary

We studied three major state management approaches in this chapter – the GetX package, the GetIt package, and Binder.

GetX is well-known for abstracting out all the core state management boilerplate code and giving the developer the ease of using readable and maintainable code. GetX uses the `GetBuilder` widget, the `GetMaterialApp` widget, and the `GetxController` class to connect code together. GetX is also very handy for neatly managing navigations in your application.

GetIt uses the `ChangeNotifier` class to reflect changes to the UI. It also uses dependency injection to make all the model classes available to the whole application. It uses the basic `setState` function to update the UI.

Binder uses scopes, state references, and view logic classes to manage states inside a Flutter application. It uses the `LogicRef` class to inject `scope` inside the `ViewLogic` class and the `StateRef` class to manage the latest values of your model classes.

The next three chapters are practical implementations of what we have studied in the last three chapters, respectively. We will learn how to create an offline shopping cart inside a Flutter application and also learn how to manage its state, using all the state management approaches we have learned in the book.

Section 3: Code-Level Implementation

In this section, you will see how to build a shopping cart application in Flutter using all the approaches defined in the previous section.

This section includes the following chapters:

6

Creating a Shopping Cart Application Using Basic Approaches

The previous chapter ended our journey of exploring and understanding the basics of different state management techniques. The next three chapters will focus on creating working examples of a simple shopping cart application containing a few screens, along with the functionality of adding and removing pre-listed items to and from the cart.

Starting from this chapter, we will see how to create a shopping cart application using `setState`, `InheritedWidget`, and `InheritedModel`.

We will be creating a two-screen application with each of the three aforementioned techniques. The first screen will display available items that can be added to the cart, while the second screen will display items that have been added to the cart. You can add/remove items to/from both screens. Both screens will be displaying the latest and updated cart items.

To be more specific, we will create the following screens for each of the techniques we studied in the previous chapters:

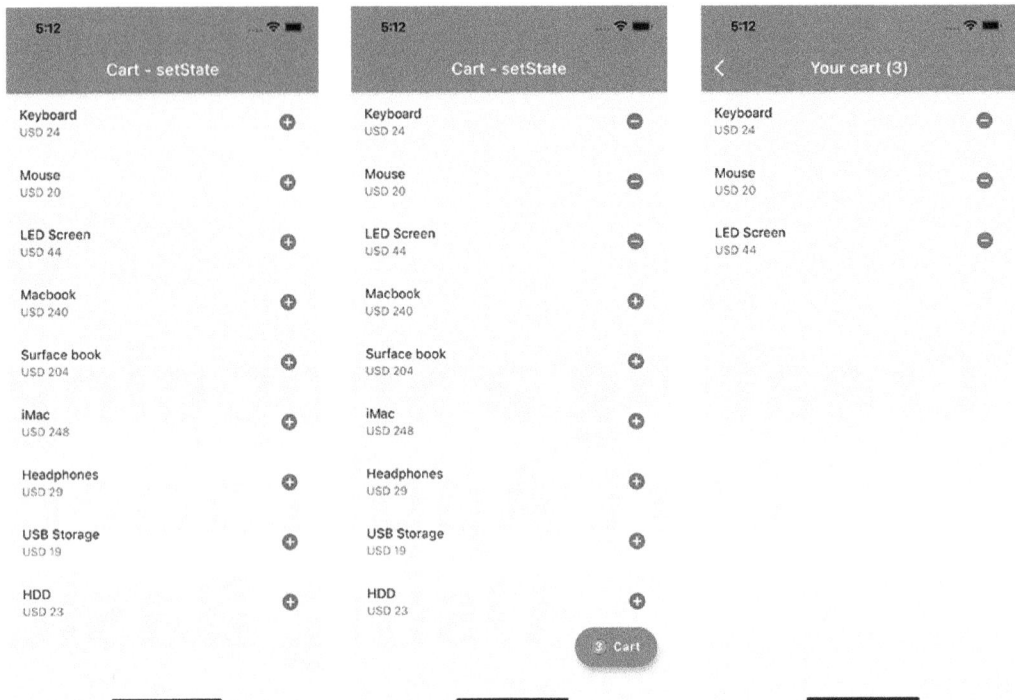

Figure 6.1 – Expected final screens

We will be discussing and implementing the following topics in this chapter:

- Creating a shopping cart application with `setState`
- Creating a shopping cart application with `InheritedWidget`
- Creating a shopping cart application with `InheritedModel`

> **Note**
>
> We are not focusing on design, **user experience** (**UX**), or complexity while creating our application. All the samples created are purely intended to develop a core understanding of how to manage state in an application that is slightly more complex than a simple counter-example application.

Let's have a quick look at the prerequisites for this chapter.

Technical requirements

In order to be able to fully understand and follow through this chapter, it is required for you to go through *Chapter 2*, *The Core Building Blocks of State Management* thoroughly beforehand. This is because we will be putting all those concepts and code keywords directly to use in this chapter.

All the code in this chapter is uploaded (in its complete form) here: `https://github.com/PacktPublishing/Managing-State-in-Flutter-Pragmatically/tree/main/ch6`.

> **Note**
>
> Since we are now advancing from beginner-level code to creating intermediate-level working applications, it is expected that you will implicitly understand and execute certain basic steps such as creating a new application, creating model classes, and adding `import` statements.

Creating a shopping cart application with setState

Without any further ado, let's jump directly into the code, as follows:

1. Create a new Flutter application in the same way as we have been doing in the previous chapters. Name this application `cart_set_state`.

2. Create a new file named `item.dart` and add a model class named `Item`, as follows:

```
class Item {
  final String? name;
  final String? price;

  Item({this.name, this.price});
}
```

3. In order to create sample data for our product list, we are creating a function that does the work for us. Add the following function below the Item class in the item.dart file:

```
List<Item> populateItems() {
  return [
    Item(name: 'Keyboard', price: '24'),
    Item(name: 'Mouse', price: '20'),
    Item(name: 'LED Screen', price: '44'),
    Item(name: 'Macbook', price: '240'),
    Item(name: 'Surface book', price: '204'),
    Item(name: 'iMac', price: '248'),
    Item(name: 'Headphones', price: '29'),
    Item(name: 'USB Storage', price: '19'),
    Item(name: 'HDD', price: '23'),
  ];
}
```

We are going to call this function inside our main.dart file in order to populate a list of items for our **user interface (UI)**.

4. In the MyHomePage class inside our main.dart file, we are going to create two separate lists of Item classes. One will be responsible for keeping the items populated by the _getItems function, and the other one will keep track of the items added to the cart. We will also add a ListView class to our UI in order to see the product list. Remove everything inside the _MyHomePageState class and add the following code:

```
late List<Item> items;
List<Item> cart = [];

void _getItems() {
  items = populateItems();
  setState(() {});
}

@override
void initState() {
  super.initState();
```

```
    _getItems();
  }
```

The late keyword is used because we know that the items will be populated before they are used. We have a list named cart that will be empty in the beginning. We are calling the _getItems function from item.dart inside our initState function.

Make sure to add an import statement for the item.dart file.

5. Let's add a build method, as follows:

```
@override
Widget build(BuildContext context) {
  return Scaffold(
    appBar: AppBar(
      title: Text(widget.title),
    ),
    body: ListView( // ListView
      children: items
          .map(
            (e) => ListTile(
              title: Text(e.name ?? ''),
              subtitle: Text("USD " + (e.price ??
              '')),
              trailing: IconButton(
                icon: Icon(
                  cart.contains(e) ? Icons.remove
                  _circle : Icons.add_circle,
                ),
                onPressed: () {
                  if (!cart.contains(e))
                    cart.add(e);
                  else
                    cart.remove(e);
                  setState(() {});
                },
              ),
            ),
          ),
        )
```

```
                .toList(),
        ),
      floatingActionButton: cart.isEmpty // Floating
      button
          ? null
          : FloatingActionButton.extended(
              onPressed: () {
                Navigator.of(context).push(
                  MaterialPageRoute(
                    builder: (context) => CartPage( //
                    Navigation
                        cart: cart,
                        onCartUpdated: (items) {
                          cart = items;
                          setState(() {});
                        }),
                  ),
                );
              },
              label: Row(
                children: [
                  Container(
                    padding: const EdgeInsets.all(4),
                    decoration: BoxDecoration(
                      shape: BoxShape.circle,
                      color: Colors.red,
                    ),
                    child: Text(cart.length.toString()),
                  ),
                  SizedBox(width: 8),
                  Text('Cart'),
                ],
              ),
            ),
    );
  }
```

There are two major parts of the UI. The first is the `ListView` class, which uses `items` to populate our product list. Each item also has an **Add/Remove** button, the icon of which turns to a - sign when the item is present in the cart and turns to a + icon when the item is not present in the cart. The second is a button that only appears when the cart has items. The **floating action button** (**FAB**) also shows the number of items that you have added to the cart.

We also navigate to a page called `CartPage`, which obviously hasn't been created yet. So, the next step is to create our cart screen, which will throw back the updated cart using a callback that is already implemented here inside `main.dart`.

6. Create a new file named `cart_page.dart` and add the following code to it:

```
import 'package:flutter/material.dart';

import 'item.dart';

class CartPage extends StatefulWidget {
  final List<Item> cart;
  final Function(List<Item>) onCartUpdated;

  CartPage({required this.cart, required
this.onCartUpdated});

  @override
  _CartPageState createState() => _CartPageState();
}

class _CartPageState extends State<CartPage> {
  @override
  Widget build(BuildContext context) {
    return Scaffold(
      appBar: AppBar(
        title: Text("Your cart
        (${widget.cart.length})"),
      ),
      body: ListView(
```

```
        children: widget.cart
            .map(
                (e) => ListTile(
                    title: Text(e.name ?? ''),
                    subtitle: Text("USD " + (e.price ??
                    '')),
                    trailing: IconButton(
                        icon: Icon(Icons.remove_circle),
                        onPressed: () {
                            widget.cart.remove(e);
                            setState(() {});
                            widget.onCartUpdated(widget.cart);
                        },
                    ),
                ),
            )
            .toList(),
        ),
    );
    }
}
```

This screen (the third screen shown in *Figure 6.1*) is pretty simple. We have a list of only those items that are added to the cart. You can also remove items from the cart, which will be reflected immediately on the list of the current screen and will also update the list on the previous screen using the callback (showing a + sign on all items that were removed from the cart screen).

Now that the `CartPage` class has been created, go back to your `main.dart` file and add an **import** statement for `cart_page.dart` at the top to get rid of errors.

Section overview

We are done with creating a cart management application using basic `setState` functionality. We have revised the following concepts from the previous chapter:

- Callbacks
- `setState` function
- Model classes

Optional challenge

Try adding a `quantity` parameter to each item. This means that your cart will now contain items with their respective quantities. There should be provisioning for updating the number of items from inside the cart.

In the next section, we are going to create the same screens using `InheritedWidget`.

Creating a shopping cart application with InheritedWidget

Let's create the same version of our shopping cart application using `InheritedWidget`. We will be reusing the code from the previous section, so it is recommended that you create a new Flutter application named `cart_inherited_widget.dart` and copy everything from the previous section's app. We'll proceed as follows:

1. First, as we did in *Chapter 2, The Core Building Blocks of State Management*, let's add the boilerplate code needed for the inherited widget state management technique. Create a new file named `inherited_widget_cart.dart` and add the following code to it:

    ```
    import 'package:flutter/material.dart';

    import 'item.dart';

    // One
    class MyCartInheritedWidget extends StatefulWidget {
      final Widget child;

      const MyCartInheritedWidget({Key? key, required
      this.child}) : super(key: key);

      static MyCartInheritedWidgetState of(BuildContext
      context) {
        final MyCartInheritedWidgetState? result =
        context.dependOnInheritedWidgetOfExactType
        <MyInheritedWidget>()!.data;

        assert(result != null, 'No counter found in
    ```

```dart
      context');
      return result!;
    }


  @override
  State<StatefulWidget> createState() {
    return MyCartInheritedWidgetState();
  }
}


class MyCartInheritedWidgetState extends
State<MyCartInheritedWidget> {
  List<Item> _items = populateItems();
  List<Item> _cart = [];


  List<Item> get items => _items;
  List<Item> get cart => _cart;

  void addToCart(Item item) {
    _cart.add(item);
    setState(() {});
  }

  void removeFromCart(Item item) {
    _cart.remove(item);
    setState(() {});
  }


  @override
  Widget build(BuildContext context) {
    return MyInheritedWidget(
      child: widget.child,
      data: this,
    );
  }
}
```

```
// Two
class MyInheritedWidget extends InheritedWidget {
  final MyCartInheritedWidgetState data;

  MyInheritedWidget({
    Key? key,
    required Widget child,
    required this.data,
  }) : super(key: key, child: child);


  @override
  bool updateShouldNotify(InheritedWidget oldWidget)
  => child != oldWidget;
}
```

The two main parts in the code block, `//One` and `//Two`, are similar to what we had in *Chapter 2, The Core Building Blocks of State Management*.

The only thing we need to focus on in this file is the `MyCartInheritedWidgetState` class where we have added variables for the original item list, the cart list, and functions that add and remove items to/from the cart. All the other code is similar to what we created in *Chapter 2, The Core Building Blocks of State Management*. Let's update our UI to use the inherited widget state management technique.

2. Inside `main.dart`, the first thing you need to do is import the `inherited_widget_cart.dart` file and then wrap your `MaterialApp` class with the inherited widget class that we just created (`MyCartInheritedWidget`), as follows:

```
class MyApp extends StatelessWidget {
  @override
  Widget build(BuildContext context) {
    return MyCartInheritedWidget( // new code
      child: MaterialApp(
        title: 'Flutter Demo',
        theme: ThemeData(
          primarySwatch: Colors.blue,
        ),
```

```
        home: MyHomePage(title: 'Flutter Demo Home
        Page'),
      ),
   );
  }
}
```

3. Let's update the _MyHomePageState class. Remove everything above the build method, including initState and the _getItems function call. We have already done that in our boilerplate code. Inside your build method, add these two lines just above the return statement:

```
@override
Widget build(BuildContext context) {
// new code
var items = MyCartInheritedWidget.of(context).items;
var cart = MyCartInheritedWidget.of(context).cart;
return Scaffold(
   appBar: AppBar(
// previous code continued … … …
```

These two lines will get you the latest values of your items and your cart and will keep on updating them automatically through the boilerplate code.

4. Let's use these two variables we created. The list inside the _MyHomePageState class will use the items variable, and the add/remove icons and the FAB will use the cart variable to update the cart and show the updated number of items in the cart respectively. The code is illustrated in the following snippet:

```
… … …
body: ListView(
   children: items // using items from within build
   method
       .map(
         (e) => ListTile(
            title: Text(e.name ?? ''),
            subtitle: Text("USD " + (e.price ?? '')),
            trailing: IconButton(
               icon: Icon(
                  cart.contains(e) ? Icons.remove_circle :
```

```
                    Icons.add_circle,
                ),
                onPressed: () {
// using cart variable to add/remove item
                if (!cart.contains(e))
// replace existing code
MyCartInheritedWidget.of(context).addToCart(e);
                else
// replace existing code
MyCartInheritedWidget.of(context).removeFromCart(e);
                setState(() {});
                },
            ),
          ),
        )
        .toList(),
),
floatingActionButton: cart.isEmpty
    ? null
    : FloatingActionButton.extended(
        onPressed: () {
          Navigator.of(context).push(
            MaterialPageRoute(
              // updated code
              builder: (context) => CartPage(),
            ),
          );
        },
        label: Row(
          children: [
            Container(
              padding: const EdgeInsets.all(4),
              decoration: BoxDecoration(
                shape: BoxShape.circle,
                color: Colors.red,
              ),
              // using cart to show the number of
```

```
                       // items
                       child: Text(cart.length.toString()),
                   ),
                   SizedBox(width: 8),
                   Text('Cart'),
               ],
           ),
       ),
```

You will notice that we don't have any callback function coming back from our
`CartPage` class now, leading to an error. This is because our boilerplate code is
going to take care of the updated `cart` variable.

5. Similarly, we will update our `CartPage` class with our inherited widget state
    management technique. Replace the contents of `cart_page.dart` with the
    following code:

```
import 'package:flutter/material.dart';

import 'inherited_widget_cart.dart';

class CartPage extends StatefulWidget {
  CartPage();

  @override
  _CartPageState createState() => _CartPageState();
}

class _CartPageState extends State<CartPage> {
  @override
  Widget build(BuildContext context) {
// using cart variable similar to main.dart
    var cart = MyCartInheritedWidget.of(context).cart;
    return Scaffold(
      appBar: AppBar(
        title: Text("Your cart (${cart.length})"),
      ),
      body: ListView(
```

```
         children: cart
            .map(
              (e) => ListTile(
                title: Text(e.name ?? ''),
                subtitle: Text("USD " + (e.price ??
                '')),
                trailing: IconButton(
                  icon: Icon(Icons.remove_circle),
                  onPressed: () {
                    MyCartInheritedWidget.of(context)
                    .removeFromCart(e);
                  },
                ),
              ),
            )
            .toList(),
        ),
      );
    }
  }
```

We have no callback function and no argument for receiving the updated `cart` variable from `main.dart`, as we are getting the updated `cart` variable directly from our boilerplate code now.

Section overview

We are finally done with implementing our shopping cart application using `InheritedWidget`. We revised the following concepts from *Chapter 2, The Core Building Blocks of State Management*:

- The boilerplate code keeps the latest state inside the variables.

- The boilerplate code updates the state using `setState` in a single place only. This makes us independent of calling `setState` everywhere in our UI.

- Wrapping up our `MaterialApp` class using our custom-created `InheritedWidget` class.

- Getting the latest state using the `.of()` method.

Optional challenge

Try adding quantity to each item. It might be easier using `InheritedWidget`. This means that your cart will now contain items, with a quantity for each. There should be provisioning for updating the number of items from inside the cart.

In the next section, we will create the same shopping cart app using `InheritedModel`.

Creating a shopping cart application with InheritedModel

This will be very similar to `InheritedWidget`, with slight changes in how we extract the latest values of the variables. Create a new app named `cart_inherited_model` and copy everything from the previous section. Then, proceed as follows:

1. Let's update our boilerplate code first. Rename the `inherited_widget_cart.dart` file `inherited_model_cart.dart`, remove all the contents, and add the following code:

    ```
    import 'package:flutter/material.dart';

    import 'item.dart';

    class MyCartInheritedModelWidget extends StatefulWidget {
      final Widget child;

      const MyCartInheritedModelWidget({Key? key, required
      this.child}) : super(key: key);

      static MyCartInheritedModelWidgetState
      of(BuildContext context) {
        final MyCartInheritedModelWidgetState? result =
            context.dependOnInheritedWidgetOfExactType
            <MyInheritedWidget>()!.data;

        assert(result != null, 'No cart found in
        context');
        return result!;
      }
    ```

```
  @override
  State<StatefulWidget> createState() {
    return MyCartInheritedModelWidgetState();
  }
}


class MyCartInheritedModelWidgetState extends
State<MyCartInheritedModelWidget> {
  List<Item> _items = populateItems();
  List<Item> _cart = [];

  List<Item> get items => _items;

  List<Item> get cart => _cart;

  void addToCart(Item item) {
    _cart.add(item);
    setState(() {});
  }

  void removeFromCart(Item item) {
    _cart.remove(item);
    setState(() {});
  }

  @override
  Widget build(BuildContext context) {
    return MyInheritedWidget(
      child: widget.child,
      data: this,
    );
  }
}

// updated code
```

```
class MyInheritedWidget extends InheritedModel<List<Item>>
{
  final MyCartInheritedModelWidgetState data;

  MyInheritedWidget({
    Key? key,
    required Widget child,
    required this.data,
  }) : super(key: key, child: child);

  @override
  bool updateShouldNotify(InheritedWidget oldWidget)
  => child != oldWidget;

  @override
  bool updateShouldNotifyDependent(covariant
  InheritedModel<List<Item>> oldWidget,
  Set<List<Item>> dependencies) {
    if (dependencies.contains(1)) return true;
    return false;
  }
}
```

Everything in this file is quite similar to the previous section's file; we have just changed the names of the classes and updated our InheritedWidget class to extend from InheritedModel<List<Item>> instead of InheritedWidget. We also have a new function inside the InheritedWidget class that checks if the dependencies have an aspect value of 1, which means the widget needs to be updated. We studied that in *Chapter 2, The Core Building Blocks of State Management*, where we specifically wanted some widgets to not rebuild when the setState function was called.

2. Let's update our UI code. Inside our main.dart file, under the _ MyHomePageState class, add the following code:

```
@override
Widget build(BuildContext context) {
  var items = MyCartInheritedModelWidget.of
  (context).items;
```

```
var cart = MyCartInheritedModelWidget.of
(context).cart;
```

These two lines remain the same; we just have our updated class name.

In the same file, under the MyApp class's build function, make a similar update, like this:

```
class MyApp extends StatelessWidget {
  @override
  Widget build(BuildContext context) {
    // updated code
    return MyCartInheritedModelWidget(
```

3. The onPressed function of the add/remove button in each list item is now using the InheritedModel class with an aspect value of 1 to update the cart, as illustrated in the following code snippet:

```
ListTile(
  title: Text(e.name ?? ''),
  subtitle: Text("USD " + (e.price ?? '')),
  trailing: IconButton(
    icon: Icon(
      cart.contains(e) ? Icons.remove_circle :
      Icons.add_circle,
    ),
    onPressed: () {
      if (!cart.contains(e))
        // replace existing code
        InheritedModel.inheritFrom<MyInheritedWidget>
        (context, aspect: 1)!.data.addToCart(e);
      else
        // replace existing code
        InheritedModel.inheritFrom<MyInheritedWidget>
        (context, aspect: 1)!.data.removeFromCart(e);
      setState(() {});
    },
  ),
),
```

The `aspect` value of 1 means that we want to update this part of the UI as soon as the `setState` function is called from within the boilerplate code.

4. Similarly, inside our `CartPage` class, we just need to update the `onPressed` function of the `remove` icon, as follows:

```
onPressed: () {
    InheritedModel.inheritFrom<MyInheritedWidget>
    (context)!.data.removeFromCart(e);
},
```

We are not passing the `aspect` value here because we don't need to, the reason being that the whole list is being updated and the whole item is being removed ultimately so that the UI is already refreshed when the corresponding item is removed.

5. Update the `cart` variable inside the `_CartPageState` class, as follows:

```
Widget build(BuildContext context) {
    // updated code
    var cart = MyCartInheritedModelWidget.of(
    context).cart;
```

Here, we have just replaced the `MyCartInheritedWidget` class with the `MyCartInheritedModelWidget` class.

Section overview

We are finally done with implementing the shopping cart application with `InheritedModel`. This was a short section because most of the code was similar to `InheritedWidget`. We revisited the idea of adding `aspect` to the `.of()` method to optimize the rebuilding of the widgets.

Summary

In this chapter, we revisited all the basics that we learned in *Chapter 2, The Core Building Blocks of State Management*. We created a shopping cart application using everything that we studied before. These are the main learning outcomes of the chapter:

- The first section covered the concepts of passing the data as arguments in screen constructors, along with passing the data back to the previous screen using callbacks.

- The second section was about adding boilerplate code so that we don't need to add `setState` calls inside our UI, making it cleaner and easier to understand.

- The third section extended the functionality of `InheritedWidget` and optimized the rebuilding of widgets using `aspect` parameters.

In the next chapter, we will learn how to create the same shopping cart application using *Provider*, *Riverpod*, **Business Logic Component** (**BLoC**), and *Cubit*. There is a high-level comparison of these techniques that we will be covering later on in *Chapter 9, Comparative State Management Analysis: When to Use What*.

7

Manipulating a Shopping Cart Application through BLoC, Provider, and React-Based Approaches

In this chapter, we will be looking into how to create a shopping cart application using the following approaches that were studied in the previous chapters:

- **Business Logic Component (BLoC)**
- Cubit
- Provider

- Riverpod
- Redux
- MobX

We will be going through all the concepts and code snippets discussed in *Chapter 3, Diving into Advanced State Management Approaches*, and *Chapter 4, Adopting State Management Approaches from React*. This chapter is longer than all other chapters as it has most of the state management approaches discussed together.

We are going to create the same screens we created in the previous chapter. These are shown again in the following screenshot:

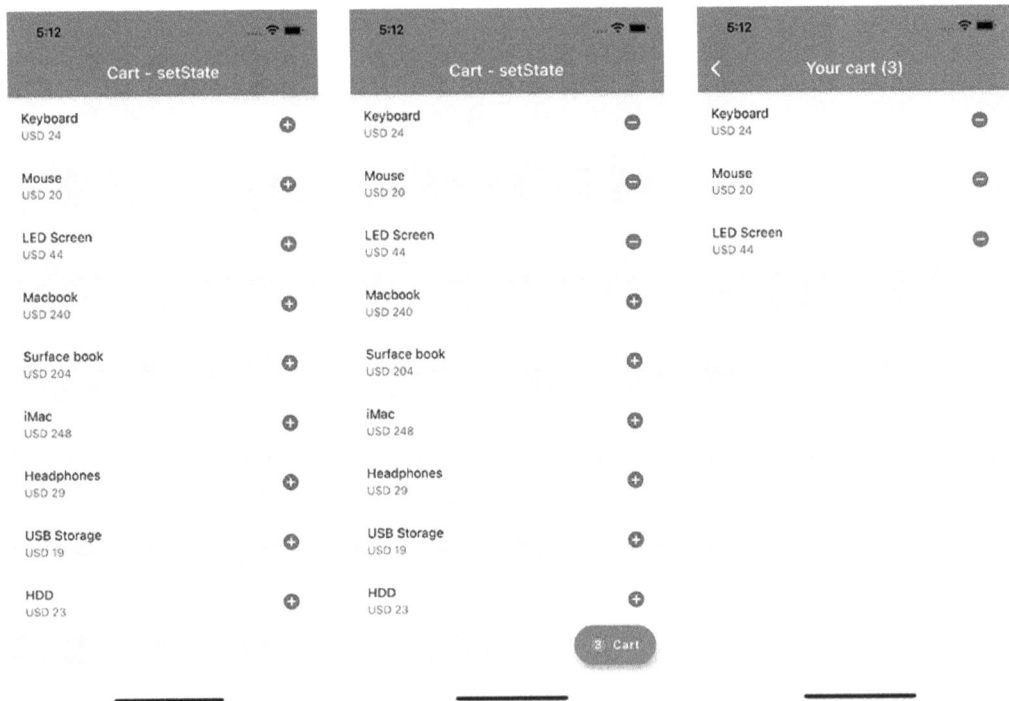

Figure 7.1 – Shopping cart application screens

Technical requirements

To be able to fully understand and follow through this chapter, it is required for you to go through *Chapter 3*, *Diving into Advanced State Management Approaches*, and *Chapter 4*, *Adopting State Management Approaches from React* thoroughly beforehand. This is because we will be putting all those concepts and code keywords directly to use in this chapter.

We will be using most of the code from the previous chapter, so it is also required that you have followed all the steps in *Chapter 6*, *Creating a Shopping Cart Application Using Basic Approaches*.

All the code in this chapter is uploaded (in its complete form) here: `https://github.com/PacktPublishing/Managing-State-in-Flutter-Pragmatically/tree/main/ch7`.

> **Note**
>
> Since we are now advancing from beginner-level code to creating intermediate-level working application, it is expected that you will implicitly understand and execute certain basic steps such as creating a new application, creating model classes, adding `import` statements, and so on.

Creating a shopping cart application with BLoC

We will be reusing the same screens we created in the previous chapter, with some editions specific to BLoC. Let's begin creating our shopping cart application using BLoC, as follows:

1. Create a new Flutter application named `cart_bloc`.
2. Copy the `item.dart` file from the previous chapter's code into the `lib` folder of your `cart_bloc` application. We will be reusing this file in all upcoming applications.

3. Create a new file named `cart_event.dart` and add the following code to it:

```
import 'item.dart';
class CartEvent {}
class AddItemToCartEvent extends CartEvent {
  final Item item;
  AddItemToCartEvent({required this.item});
}
class RemoveItemFromCartEvent extends CartEvent {
  final Item item;
  RemoveItemFromCartEvent({required this.item});
}
```

We created two events for our cart, one for adding an item to the cart and one for removing an item from the cart.

4. Create a new file named `cart_state.dart` and add the following code to it:

```
import 'package:equatable/equatable.dart';
import 'item.dart';

class CartState extends Equatable {
  final List<Item> cart;
  CartState({this.cart = const []});
  @override
  List<Object?> get props => [this.cart];
}
class CartUpdatingState {}
```

You will have to add the dependency for the `equatable` package from `pub.dev`.

5. Create a new file named `cart_bloc.dart` and add the following code to it:

```
import 'package:cart_bloc/item.dart';
import 'package:flutter_bloc/flutter_bloc.dart';
import 'cart_event.dart';
import 'cart_state.dart';

class CartBloc extends Bloc {
  CartBloc() : super(initialState);
```

```
    static get initialState => CartState();
    List<Item> items = populateItems();
    List<Item> cart = [];
    @override
    Stream mapEventToState(event) async* {
      yield CartUpdatingState();
      if (event is AddItemToCartEvent) {
        cart.add(event.item);
        yield CartState(cart: cart);
      }
      if (event is RemoveItemFromCartEvent) {
        cart.remove(event.item);
        yield CartState(cart: cart);
      }
    }
  }
```

This is quite similar to what we did in *Chapter 3, Diving into Advanced State Management Approaches,* for creating a counter application. We have two checks for events, and we perform the addition/removal of an item to/from the list accordingly. We have two lists—one is an `items` list that is not going to change and is being used to populate the items on the first screen, and the other is a `cart` list that will be updated as the user adds/removes items to/from the cart.

You will have to add the dependency for the `flutter_bloc` package from `pub.dev`.

6. Inside `main.dart`, remove everything from the `_MyHomePageState` class, and add the following code:

```
@override
Widget build(BuildContext context) {
  // One
  var items = BlocProvider.of<CartBloc>(
context).items;
  return BlocBuilder(
      bloc: BlocProvider.of<CartBloc>(context),
      builder: (context, snapshot) {
        // Two
```

```
        var cart = (snapshot as CartState).cart;
    if (snapshot is CartState)
      return Scaffold(
        appBar: AppBar(
          title: Text(widget.title),
        ),
        body: ListView(
          children: items
              .map(
                (e) => ListTile(
                  title: Text(e.name ?? ''),
                  subtitle: Text("USD " + (
                  e.price ?? '')),
                  trailing: IconButton(
                    icon: Icon(
                      cart.contains(e) ?
                      Icons.remove_circle :
                      Icons.add_circle,
                    ),
                    onPressed: () {
                      if (!snapshot.cart
                      .contains(e))

// Three

                        BlocProvider.of<CartBloc>
                        (context).add(
                        AddItemToCartEvent(
                        item: e));
                      else
                        BlocProvider.of<CartBloc>(
                        context).add(
                        RemoveItemFromCartEvent(
                        item: e));
                    },
                  ),
                ),
```

```
                    )
                  .toList(),
            ),
        floatingActionButton:
        snapshot.cart.isEmpty
              ? null
              : FloatingActionButton.extended(
                  onPressed: () {
                    Navigator.of(context).push(
                      MaterialPageRoute(
                        builder: (context) =>
                        CartPage(),
                      ),
                    );
                  },
                  label: Row(
                    children: [
                      Container(
                        padding: const
                        EdgeInsets.all(4),
                        decoration: BoxDecoration(
                          shape: BoxShape.circle,
                          color: Colors.red,
                        ),
                        child: Text(snapshot.cart.
                        length.toString()),
                      ),
                      SizedBox(width: 8),
                      Text('Cart'),
                    ],
                  ),
                ),
          );
        return Container();
    });
}
```

Section One: We are getting a list of items to be shown directly from our BLoC class using `BuildContext`. We don't need to put it under `BlocBuilder`.

Section Two: We pick up our latest `cart` variable from the latest state that is updated whenever the user adds/removes an item to/from the cart.

Section Three: We add events for the addition/removal of items to our BLoC class.

Make sure to add missing `import` statements at the top, as follows:

```
import 'package:flutter_bloc/flutter_bloc.dart';


import 'cart_bloc.dart';
import 'cart_event.dart';
import 'cart_state.dart';
import 'cart_page.dart.dart';
```

We have a `FloatingActionButton` class, just as in the previous chapter, which is responsible for showing the latest count of items added inside the cart and for navigating to the cart screen (for reference, check out the first two screens shown in *Figure 7.1*).

7. Create a new file named `cart_page.dart` and add the following code to it:

```
import 'package:flutter/material.dart';
import 'package:flutter_bloc/flutter_bloc.dart';
import 'cart_bloc.dart';
import 'cart_event.dart';
import 'cart_state.dart';

class CartPage extends StatefulWidget {
  CartPage();
  @override
  _CartPageState createState() => _CartPageState();
}

class _CartPageState extends State<CartPage> {
  @override
  Widget build(BuildContext context) {
    return BlocBuilder(
        bloc: BlocProvider.of<CartBloc>(context),
        builder: (context, snapshot) {
```

```
          if (snapshot is CartState)
            return Scaffold(
              appBar: AppBar(
                title: Text("Your cart
                (${snapshot.cart.length})"),
              ),
              body: ListView(
                children: snapshot.cart
                    .map(
                        (e) => ListTile(
                          title: Text(e.name ?? ''),
                          subtitle: Text("USD " +
                          (e.price ?? '')),
                          trailing: IconButton(
                            icon: Icon(
                            Icons.remove_circle),
                            onPressed: () {
                              BlocProvider.of<CartBloc>
                              (context).add
                              (RemoveItemFromCartEvent(
                              item: e));
                            },
                          ),
                        ),
                    )
                    .toList(),
              ),
            );
          return Container();
        });
  }
}
```

This class is very similar to the same cart page we created in the previous chapter, with the addition of picking up the latest cart items from the snapshot and adding an event for removing an item from the cart (for reference, check out the last screen shown in *Figure 7.1*).

8. The last step is to wrap your `MaterialApp` class with a `MultiBlocProvider` class, as we did in *Chapter 3, Diving into Advanced State Management Approaches*. The code is illustrated in the following snippet:

```
class MyApp extends StatelessWidget {
  @override
  Widget build(BuildContext context) {
    return MultiBlocProvider(
      providers: [
        BlocProvider<CartBloc>(create: (context) =>
        CartBloc()),
      ],
      child: MaterialApp(
        title: 'Flutter Demo',
        theme: ThemeData(
          primarySwatch: Colors.blue,
        ),
        home: MyHomePage(title: 'Cart - Bloc'),
      ),
    );
  }
}
```

Make sure to add missing `import` statements at the top, as follows:

```
import 'cart_page.dart';
```

And you are done with your shopping cart app using BLoC state management. If you have studied the concepts of BLoC in *Chapter 3, Diving into Advanced State Management Approaches*, this should have been easy for you. If you are still struggling with the code, don't worry. You will definitely get a grasp of it gradually. Besides, you might want to revisit the previous conceptual chapters where we studied basic forms of every technique.

The next section is about creating a shopping cart application using Cubit, which—as we studied earlier—is a variation of BLoC.

Creating a shopping cart application with Cubit

Cubit is a slight variant of BLoC. To create a shopping cart application using Cubit, create a new Flutter application named `cart_cubit` and copy `item.dart` and `cart_state.dart` from the previous section's application into your `lib` folder. Also, add dependencies for the `equatable` and `flutter_bloc` packages from `pub.dev`. Then, follow these steps:

1. Replace the contents of the `cart_state.dart` file with the following code:

```
import 'package:equatable/equatable.dart';
import 'item.dart';

class CartState extends Equatable {
  @override
  List<Object?> get props => [];
}
class CartListState extends CartState {
  final List<Item> cart;
  CartListState({this.cart = const []});
  @override
  List<Object?> get props => [this.cart];
}


class CartUpdatingState extends CartState {}
```

2. Create a new file named `cart_cubit.dart` and add the following code to it:

```
import 'cart_state.dart';
import 'package:flutter_bloc/flutter_bloc.dart';
import 'item.dart';
class CartCubit extends Cubit<CartState> {
  CartCubit() : super(initialState);
  static get initialState => CartListState();
  List<Item> items = populateItems();
  List<Item> cart = [];
  addItemToCart(Item item) async {
    emit(CartUpdatingState());
    cart.add(item);
```

```
      emit(CartListState(cart: cart));
  }

  removeItemFromCart(Item item) async {
    emit(CartUpdatingState());
    cart.remove(item);
    emit(CartListState(cart: cart));
  }
}
```

This is very similar to what we did in BLoC, but instead of events, we have direct functions for adding items to and removing items from the cart.

3. Inside main.dart, remove everything from the _MyHomePageState class, and add the following code:

```
@override
Widget build(BuildContext context) {
  var items = BlocProvider.of<CartCubit>
  (context).items;
  return BlocBuilder(
      bloc: BlocProvider.of<CartCubit>(context),
      builder: (context, snapshot) {
        var cart = (snapshot as CartListState).cart;
        if (snapshot is CartListState)
          return Scaffold(
            appBar: AppBar(
              title: Text(widget.title),
            ),
            body: ListView(
              children: items
                  .map(
                    (e) => ListTile(
                      title: Text(e.name ?? ''),
                      subtitle: Text("USD " + (e.price
                      ?? '')),
                      trailing: IconButton(
                        icon: Icon(
```

```
                    cart.contains(e) ? Icons.
                    remove_circle : Icons.add
                    _circle,
                  ),
                  onPressed: () {
                    if (!snapshot.cart
                    .contains(e))
```

```
// Updated code
                        BlocProvider.of<CartCubit>
                        (context).addItemToCart(e);
                        else
                           BlocProvider.of<CartCubit>
                           (context).
                           removeItemFromCart(e);
                      },
                    ),
                  ),
                )
                .toList(),
            ),
        floatingActionButton:
        snapshot.cart.isEmpty
            ? null
            : FloatingActionButton.extended(
                onPressed: () {
                  Navigator.of(context).push(
                    MaterialPageRoute(
                      builder: (context) =>
                      CartPage(),
                    ),
                  );
                },
                label: Row(
                  children: [
                    Container(
```

```
                    padding: const
                    EdgeInsets.all(4),
                    decoration: BoxDecoration(
                      shape: BoxShape.circle,
                      color: Colors.red,
                    ),
                    child: Text(snapshot.cart.
                    length.toString()),
                  ),
                  SizedBox(width: 8),
                  Text('Cart'),
                ],
              ),
            ),
          );
      return Container();
    });
}
```

Make sure to add missing import statements at the top, as follows:

```
import 'package:flutter_bloc/flutter_bloc.dart';
import 'cart_cubit.dart';
import 'cart_state.dart';
```

This code is exactly the same as for BLoC; the only difference is the way item addition/removal functions are called (for reference, check out the first two screens shown in *Figure 7.1*).

4. The cart_page.dart file also remains the same, with very minor changes. Create a new file named cart_page.dart and add the following code to it:

```
import 'package:flutter/material.dart';
import 'package:flutter_bloc/flutter_bloc.dart';
import 'cart_cubit.dart';
import 'cart_state.dart';

class CartPage extends StatefulWidget {
  CartPage();
  @override
```

```
    _CartPageState createState() => _CartPageState();
}


class _CartPageState extends State<CartPage> {
  @override
  Widget build(BuildContext context) {
    return BlocBuilder(
        bloc: BlocProvider.of<CartCubit>(context),
        builder: (context, snapshot) {
          if (snapshot is CartListState)
            return Scaffold(
              appBar: AppBar(
                title: Text("Your cart
                (${snapshot.cart.length})"),
              ),
              body: ListView(
                children: snapshot.cart
                  .map(
                    (e) => ListTile(
                      title: Text(e.name ?? ''),
                      subtitle: Text("USD " +
                      (e.price ?? '')),
                      trailing: IconButton(
                        icon: Icon(
                        Icons.remove_circle),
                        onPressed: () {

// Updated code

                          BlocProvider.of
                          <CartCubit>(context)
                          .removeItemFromCart(e);
                        },
                      ),
                    ),
                  )
                  .toList(),
```

```
            ),
          );
        return Container();
      });
  }
}
```

(For reference, check out the last screen shown in *Figure 7.1.*)

5. Your `MaterialApp` class will be wrapped with `MultiBlocProvider` as usual, as illustrated in the following code snippet:

```
class MyApp extends StatelessWidget {
  @override
  Widget build(BuildContext context) {
    return MultiBlocProvider(
      providers: [
        BlocProvider<CartCubit>(
          create: (context) => CartCubit(),
        ),
      ],
      child: MaterialApp(
        title: 'Flutter Demo',
        theme: ThemeData(
          primarySwatch: Colors.blue,
        ),
        home: MyHomePage(title: 'Flutter Demo Home
        Page'),
      ),
    );
  }
}
```

Make sure to add missing `import` statements at the top, as follows:

```
import 'cart_page.dart';
```

And there you go. In four simple steps, you are done with your shopping cart application using Cubit state management!

In the next section, we will see how to create a shopping cart application using Provider state management.

Creating a shopping cart application with Provider

Create a new Flutter application named `cart_provider` and copy `item.dart` into your `lib` folder, as we have been doing in the previous sections. Also, add dependencies for Provider from `pub.dev`. Let's get started, as follows:

1. Create a new file named `cart_model.dart` and add the following code to it:

    ```
    import 'item.dart';
    import 'package:flutter/material.dart';

    class Cart with ChangeNotifier {
      List<Item> _items = populateItems();
      List<Item> _cart = [];
      List<Item> get items => _items;
      List<Item> get cart => _cart;
      void addToCart(Item item) {
        _cart.add(item);
        notifyListeners();
      }

      void removeFromCart(Item item) {
        _cart.remove(item);
        notifyListeners();
      }
    }
    ```

As we studied in *Chapter 3, Diving into Advanced State Management Approaches*, Provider uses the `ChangeNotifier` class to notify its listeners using the `notifyListeners` function. We have added two separate functions to add items to and remove items from the cart, each with a call to the `notifyListeners` function.

2. Inside `main.dart`, remove everything from the `_MyHomePageState` class, and add the following code:

```dart
@override
Widget build(BuildContext context) {
  var items = context.watch<Cart>().items;
  var cart = context.watch<Cart>().cart;
  return Scaffold(
    appBar: AppBar(
      title: Text(widget.title),
    ),
    body: ListView(
      children: items
          .map(
            (e) => ListTile(
              title: Text(e.name ?? ''),
              subtitle: Text("USD " + (e.price ??
              '')),
              trailing: IconButton(
                icon: Icon(
                  cart.contains(e) ? Icons.remove
                  _circle : Icons.add_circle,
                ),
                onPressed: () {
                  if (!cart.contains(e))
                    context.read<Cart>().addToCart(e);
                  else
                    context.read<Cart>()
                    .removeFromCart(e);
                },
              ),
            ),
          )
          .toList(),
    ),
    floatingActionButton: cart.isEmpty
```

```
          ? null
          : FloatingActionButton.extended(
              onPressed: () {
                Navigator.of(context).push(
                  MaterialPageRoute(
                    builder: (context) => CartPage(),
                  ),
                );
              },
              label: Row(
                children: [
                  Container(
                    padding: const EdgeInsets.all(4),
                    decoration: BoxDecoration(
                      shape: BoxShape.circle,
                      color: Colors.red,
                    ),
                    child: Text(cart.length.toString()),
                  ),
                  SizedBox(width: 8),
                  Text('Cart'),
                ],
              ),
            ),
  );
}
```

Make sure to add missing import statements at the top, as follows:

```
import 'package:provider/provider.dart';
import 'cart_model.dart';
```

This is very similar to all the main pages we have been looking at in previous sections. The only difference is how we fetch the items and cart variables. Here, in this example, we fetch them through the context.watch function, which allows us to retrieve variables through the context (for reference, check out the first two screens shown in *Figure 7.1*).

3. The `cart_page.dart` file also uses the `context.watch` function to get the latest cart items. Create a new file named `cart_page.dart` and add the following code to it:

```
import 'package:cart_provider/cart_model.dart';
import 'package:flutter/material.dart';
import 'package:provider/provider.dart';

class CartPage extends StatefulWidget {
  CartPage();

  @override
  _CartPageState createState() => _CartPageState();
}

class _CartPageState extends State<CartPage> {
  @override
  Widget build(BuildContext context) {
    var cart = context.watch<Cart>().cart;
    return Scaffold(
      appBar: AppBar(
        title: Text("Your cart (${cart.length})"),
      ),
      body: ListView(
        children: cart
            .map(
              (e) => ListTile(
                title: Text(e.name ?? ''),
                subtitle: Text("USD " + (e.price ??
                '')),
                trailing: IconButton(
```

```
                        icon: Icon(Icons.remove_circle),
                        onPressed: () {
                          context.read<Cart>()
                          .removeFromCart(e);
                        },
                      ),
                    ),
                  )
                .toList(),
              ),
            );
          }
        }
```

(For reference, check out the last screen shown in *Figure 7.1*.)

Make sure to add missing `import` statements at the top of the `main.dart` file to remove all errors, as follows:

```
import cart_page.dart';
```

Lastly, update your `main` function inside the `main.dart` file to use `ChangeNotifierProvider`, wrapping up your `MyApp` class, as follows:

```
void main() {
  runApp(ChangeNotifierProvider<Cart>(
    child: MyApp(),
    create: (_) => Cart(),
  ));
}
```

We are done with creating a shopping cart application using Provider. This gets easier if you have studied and followed the steps in the early chapters.

In the next section, we are going to see how to create a shopping cart application using Riverpod.

Creating a shopping cart application with Riverpod

Create a new Flutter app named `cart_riverpod` and copy `item.dart` into your `lib` folder, as we have been doing in the previous sections. Add dependencies for `equatable` and `flutter_riverpod` from `pub.dev`. Let's get started, as follows:

1. Create a new file named `cart_model.dart` and add the following code to it:

```dart
import 'item.dart';
import 'package:flutter_riverpod/flutter_riverpod.dart';

final cartProvider = StateNotifierProvider((ref) =>
CartNotifier());

class CartNotifier extends StateNotifier<CartModel> {
  CartNotifier() : super(CartModel(cart: []));

  void addToCart(Item item) {
    var updatedCart = state.cart;
    updatedCart.add(item);
    state = CartModel(cart: updatedCart);
  }

  void removeFromCart(Item item) {
    var updatedCart = state.cart;
    updatedCart.remove(item);
    state = CartModel(cart: updatedCart);
  }
}

class CartModel {
  CartModel({required this.cart});
  List<Item> _items = populateItems();
  List<Item> get items => _items;
  List<Item> cart;
}
```

Recalling what we studied in *Chapter 3, Diving into Advanced State Management Approaches,* about Riverpod, we have the concept of state notifiers, which are a part of state notifier providers. Therefore, we have created a global provider that keeps CartNotifier. CartNotifier extends a StateNotifier notifier of type CartModel that keeps a list of items in the cart. The CartNotifier is also responsible for updating items in the cart as the user triggers its functions.

2. Inside main.dart, remove everything inside the _MyHomePageState class, and add the following code:

```
@override
Widget build(BuildContext context) {
  return Consumer(builder: (context, watch, _) {
    final state = watch(cartProvider) as CartModel;
    var items = state.items;
    var cart = state.cart;
    return Scaffold(
      appBar: AppBar(
        title: Text(widget.title),
      ),
      body: ListView(
        children: items
            .map(
              (e) => ListTile(
                title: Text(e.name ?? ''),
                subtitle: Text("USD " + (e.price ??
                '')),
                trailing: IconButton(
                  icon: Icon(
                    cart.contains(e) ? Icons.remove
                    _circle : Icons.add_circle,
                  ),
                  onPressed: () {
                    if (!cart.contains(e))
                      context.read(
                      cartProvider.notifier)
                      .addToCart(e);
```

```
                    else
                      context.read(
                      cartProvider.notifier)
                      .removeFromCart(e);
                  },
                ),
              ),
            )
          .toList(),
      ),
    floatingActionButton: cart.isEmpty
        ? null
        : FloatingActionButton.extended(
            onPressed: () {
              Navigator.of(context).push(
                MaterialPageRoute(
                  builder: (context) => CartPage(),
                ),
              );
            },
            label: Row(
              children: [
                Container(
                  padding: const EdgeInsets.all(4),
                  decoration: BoxDecoration(
                    shape: BoxShape.circle,
                    color: Colors.red,
                  ),
                  child: Text(
                  cart.length.toString())),
                ),
                SizedBox(width: 8),
                Text('Cart'),
              ],
            ),
          ),
```

```
      );
    });
  }
```

Make sure to add missing imports at the top, as follows:

```
import 'package:flutter_riverpod/flutter_riverpod.dart';
import 'cart_model.dart';
```

Here, the Consumer widget does the job for us by fetching the latest state of CartModel using the watch function. The read functions are used to trigger the addition/removal of items to and from the cart (for reference, check out the first two screens shown in *Figure 7.1*).

3.   The cart_page.dart file also uses watch and read functions to fetch and update the cart variable respectively. Create a new file named cart_page.dart and add the following code to it:

```
import 'cart_model.dart';
import 'package:flutter/material.dart';
import 'package:flutter_riverpod/flutter_riverpod.dart';


class CartPage extends StatefulWidget {
  CartPage();

  @override
  _CartPageState createState() => _CartPageState();
}


class _CartPageState extends State<CartPage> {
  @override
  Widget build(BuildContext context) {
    return Consumer(builder: (context, watch, _) {
      final state = watch(cartProvider) as CartModel;
      var cart = state.cart;
      return Scaffold(
        appBar: AppBar(
          title: Text("Your cart (${cart.length})"),
        ),
        body: ListView(
```

```
            children: cart
                .map(
                    (e) => ListTile(
                        title: Text(e.name ?? ''),
                        subtitle: Text("USD " + (e.price ??
                        '')),
                        trailing: IconButton(
                            icon: Icon(Icons.remove_circle),
                            onPressed: () {
                                context.read(
                                cartProvider.notifier)
                                .removeFromCart(e);
                            },
                        ),
                    ),
                )
                .toList(),
        ),
    );
  });
  }
}
```

Make sure to add missing imports at the top of the `main.dart` file to remove all errors, as follows:

```
import cart_page.dart';
```

(For reference, check out the last screen shown in *Figure 7.1*.)

Lastly, update your `main` function inside the `main.dart` file to use `ProviderScope`, wrapping up your `MyApp` class, as follows:

```
void main() {
    runApp(ProviderScope(child: MyApp()));
}
```

We are done with creating a shopping cart application using Riverpod.

In the next section, we will discuss how to create a shopping cart application using Redux state management.

Creating a shopping cart application with Redux

Create a new Flutter application named `cart_redux` and copy `item.dart` into your `lib` folder, as we have been doing in the previous sections. Add dependencies for `equatable` and `flutter_redux` from `pub.dev`. Let's get started, as follows:

1. Create a new file named `actions.dart` and add the following code to it:

```
import 'item.dart';


class Actions {}


class AddItemToCartAction extends Actions {
  final Item item;
  AddItemToCartAction({required this.item});
}


class RemoveItemFromCartAction extends Actions {
  final Item item;
  RemoveItemFromCartAction({required this.item});
}
```

Both of these actions are self-explanatory; we will be using these to trigger the addition/removal of items to and from the cart.

2. Create a file named `cart_state.dart` and add the following code to it:

```
import 'package:equatable/equatable.dart';
import 'package:redux/redux.dart';
import 'actions.dart';
import 'item.dart';


class CartState extends Equatable {
  final List<Item> cart;
  CartState({this.cart = const []});
  @override
  List<Object?> get props => [this.cart];
}
```

```
CartState cartReducer(CartState state, dynamic action) {
  if (action is AddItemToCartAction) {
    var updatedCart = <Item>[];
    updatedCart.addAll(state.cart);
    updatedCart.add(action.item);
    return CartState(cart: updatedCart);
  }

  if (action is RemoveItemFromCartAction) {
    var updatedCart = <Item>[];
    updatedCart.addAll(state.cart);
    updatedCart.remove(action.item);
    return CartState(cart: updatedCart);
  }

  return state;
}
final store = Store<CartState>(cartReducer, initialState:
CartState());
final items = populateItems();
```

As we studied in Redux, we have a `reducer` function that handles the state and actions triggered by the **user interface (UI)**. In this file, we also created a global `store` variable, which is the crux of Redux state management (single source of state). We also added a global variable for `items` because that is our static data, which is never going to change.

3. In `main.dart`, remove everything inside the `_MyHomePageState` class and add the following code:

```
@override
Widget build(BuildContext context) {
  // One
  return StoreConnector<CartState, List<Item>>(
      converter: (store) => store.state.cart,
      builder: (context, cart) {
        return Scaffold(
          appBar: AppBar(
            title: Text(widget.title),
```

```
        ),
      body: ListView(
        children: items
            .map(
              (e) => ListTile(
                title: Text(e.name ?? ''),
                subtitle: Text("USD " + (e.price
                ?? '')),
                trailing: IconButton(
                  icon: Icon(
                    cart.contains(e) ?
                    Icons.remove_circle :
                    Icons.add_circle,
                  ),
                  onPressed: () {
                    if (!cart.contains(e))
```

// Two

```
                      store.dispatch(
                      AddItemToCartAction(
                      item: e));
                    else
                      store.dispatch(
                      RemoveItemFromCartAction(
                      item: e));
                  },
                ),
              ),
            )
            .toList(),
      ),
      floatingActionButton: cart.isEmpty
          ? null
          : FloatingActionButton.extended(
            onPressed: () {
              Navigator.of(context).push(
```

```
                    MaterialPageRoute(
                      builder: (context) =>
                      CartPage(),
                    ),
                  );
                },
                label: Row(
                  children: [
                    Container(
                      padding: const
                      EdgeInsets.all(4),
                      decoration: BoxDecoration(
                        shape: BoxShape.circle,
                        color: Colors.red,
                      ),
                      child: Text(
                      cart.length.toString()),
                    ),
                    SizedBox(width: 8),
                    Text('Cart'),
                  ],
                ),
              ),
            );
          return Container();
        });
}
```

Section One: We have our `StoreConnector` widget that is responsible for listening to changes done by our `reducer` function. This gives us an updated `cart` variable after every action performed by the user.

Section Two: The `dispatch` function inside our store is responsible for triggering actions to add/remove items to and from the cart (for reference, check out the first two screens shown in *Figure 7.1*).

Make sure to add missing `import` statements at the top, as follows:

```
import 'package:flutter_redux/flutter_redux.dart';
import 'actions.dart';
import 'cart_state.dart';
import 'item.dart';
```

4. Create a new file named `cart_page.dart` and add the following code, which is very similar to the `cart_page.dart` file from the previous sections:

```
import 'package:flutter/material.dart';
import 'package:flutter_redux/flutter_redux.dart';
import 'actions.dart';
import 'cart_state.dart';
import 'item.dart';


class CartPage extends StatefulWidget {
  CartPage();
  @override
  _CartPageState createState() => _CartPageState();
}


class _CartPageState extends State<CartPage> {
  @override
  Widget build(BuildContext context) {
    return StoreConnector<CartState, List<Item>>(
      converter: (store) => store.state.cart,
      builder: (context, cart) {
        return Scaffold(
          appBar: AppBar(
            title: Text("Your cart
            (${cart.length})"),
          ),
          body: ListView(
            children: cart
```

```
                          .map(
                            (e) => ListTile(
                              title: Text(e.name ?? ''),
                              subtitle: Text("USD " + (e.price
                              ?? '')),
                              trailing: IconButton(
                                icon: Icon(
                                Icons.remove_circle),
                                onPressed: () {
                                  store.dispatch(
                                  RemoveItemFromCartAction(
                                  item: e));
                                },
                              ),
                            ),
                          )
                          .toList(),
                        ),
                      );
                    return Container();
                });
              }
            }
```

We have a `StoreConnector` widget and a `dispatch` function for triggering an action, just as in our `main.dart` file (for reference, check out the last screen shown in *Figure 7.1*).

5. Finally, we just need to wrap our application with a `StoreProvider` class. Inside the `main.dart` file, update your `runApp` function, as follows:

```
runApp(
  StoreProvider(
    child: MyApp(),
    store: store,
  ),
);
```

Make sure to add missing `import` statements at the top of the file to remove all errors, as follows:

```
import cart_page.dart';
```

And we are done with implementing a shopping cart management application using Redux state management.

The next (and last) section of this chapter is about creating a shopping cart application using MobX.

Creating a shopping cart application with MobX

Create a new Flutter application named `cart_mobx` and copy `item.dart` into your `lib` folder, as we have been doing in the previous sections. Add dependencies for `equitable`, `flutter_mobx`, and `mobx` under dependencies inside `pubspec.yaml`. Also, add dependencies for `build_runner` and `mobx_codegen` under dev_dependencies in `pubspec.yaml`. Let's get started, as follows:

1. Create a new file named `cart.dart` and add the following code to it:

    ```
    import 'package:mobx/mobx.dart';

    import 'item.dart';

    part 'cart.g.dart';

    class Cart = _Cart with _$Cart;

    abstract class _Cart with Store {
      List<Item> items = populateItems();

      @observable
      List<Item> cart = [];

      @action
      void addItemToCart(Item item) {
    ```

```
    var newCart = <Item>[];
    newCart.addAll(cart);
    newCart.add(item);
    cart = newCart;
  }

  @action
  removeItemFromCart(Item item) {
    var newCart = <Item>[];
    newCart.addAll(cart);
    newCart.remove(item);
    cart = newCart;
  }
}
```

We have a normal `List` variable that is not observable because that is the static items' list, and we have an observable list, which is our `cart` variable. We have two observable functions for adding an item to and removing an item from the cart. The part `'cart.g.dart'` line will give an error because that file doesn't exist right now. We studied in *Chapter 4, Adopting State Management Approaches from React,* that MobX uses autogenerated code using a command related to `build_runner` dependency, so we are going to generate that now.

2. Open the terminal window inside your **integrated development environment (IDE)** and run the following command:

```
flutter packages pub run build_runner build --delete-
conflicting-outputs
```

This will generate the required state management code that will be used by the MobX dependency.

3. In `main.dart`, remove everything inside the `_MyHomePageState` class and add the following code:

```
@override
Widget build(BuildContext context) {
  return Observer(builder: (_) {
    return Scaffold(
      appBar: AppBar(
```

```
            title: Text(widget.title),
          ),
          body: ListView(
            children: cart.items
                .map(
                    (e) => ListTile(
                      title: Text(e.name ?? ''),
                      subtitle: Text("USD " + (e.price ??
                      '')),
                      trailing: IconButton(
                        icon: Icon(
                          cart.cart.contains(e) ?
                          Icons.remove_circle :
                          Icons.add_circle,
                        ),
                        onPressed: () {
                          if (!cart.cart.contains(e))
                            cart.addItemToCart(e);
                          else
                            cart.removeItemFromCart(e);
                        },
                      ),
                    ),
                )
                .toList(),
          ),
          floatingActionButton: cart.cart.isEmpty
              ? null
              : FloatingActionButton.extended(
                  onPressed: () {
                    Navigator.of(context).push(
                      MaterialPageRoute(
                        builder: (context) => CartPage(),
                      ),
                    );
                  },
```

```
                    label: Row(
                      children: [
                        Container(
                          padding: const EdgeInsets.all(4),
                          decoration: BoxDecoration(
                            shape: BoxShape.circle,
                            color: Colors.red,
                          ),
                          child: Text(
                          cart.cart.length.toString()),
                        ),
                        SizedBox(width: 8),
                        Text('Cart'),
                      ],
                    ),
                  ),
              );
          return Container();
        });
    }
```

Add the following line outside the class globally:

```
final Cart cart = Cart();
```

Make sure to add missing import statements at the top, as follows:

```
import 'package:flutter_mobx/flutter_mobx.dart';
import 'cart.dart';
```

We have an `Observer` widget at the top of our widget hierarchy; this observer is responsible for listening to changes done by MobX autogenerated code. We are also calling add/remove functions directly using our global `cart` variable (for reference, check out the first two screens shown in *Figure 7.1*).

4. Create a new file named `cart_page.dart` and add the following code to it:

```
import 'package:flutter/material.dart';
import 'package:flutter_mobx/flutter_mobx.dart';
import 'main.dart';
```

```dart
class CartPage extends StatefulWidget {
  CartPage();
  @override
  _CartPageState createState() => _CartPageState();
}


class _CartPageState extends State<CartPage> {
  @override
  Widget build(BuildContext context) {
    return Observer(builder: (_) {
      return Scaffold(
        appBar: AppBar(
          title: Text("Your cart
          (${cart.cart.length})"),
        ),
        body: ListView(
          children: cart.cart
            .map(
              (e) => ListTile(
                title: Text(e.name ?? ''),
                subtitle: Text("USD " + (e.price ??
                '')),
                trailing: IconButton(
                  icon: Icon(Icons.remove_circle),
                  onPressed: () {
                    cart.removeItemFromCart(e);
                  },
                ),
              ),
            )
            .toList(),
        ),
      );
    });
  }
}
```

The `cart` page also uses the `Observer` widget to listen to state changes. It uses the same global `cart` variable to call the remove function (for reference, check out the last screen shown in *Figure 7.1*).

Make sure to add missing `import` statements at the top of the `main.dart` file to remove all errors, as follows:

```
import cart_page.dart';
```

And here we are at the end of the chapter, done with creating shopping cart applications using MobX state management.

Summary

This chapter was full of code snippets, where we created a shopping cart application using six different state management techniques that we studied in a couple of previous chapters—*BLoC, Cubit, Provider, Riverpod, Redux*, and *MobX*.

This chapter was a deep dive into all of those six techniques discussed in the previous chapters. We have practically implemented all the concepts of all the aforementioned techniques, which include *events, states*, and *actions* in *BLoC* and *Cubit*; usage of the `.of()` method in *Provider* and *Riverpod*; the single source of true state in *Redux*; and code autogeneration in *MobX*. Furthermore, by now, you should have completely understood the following state management techniques—`setState`, `InheritedWidget`, `InheritedModel`, *Provider, Riverpod, BLoC, Cubit, Redux*, and *MobX*.

In the next chapter, we will study how to create a shopping cart application using *GetX*, *GetIt*, and *Binder* state management techniques.

8
Using GetX, GetIt, and Binder to Update the Cart Application

In this chapter, we will be looking into how to create a cart application using the following approaches, which were studied in the previous chapters:

- GetX
- GetIt
- Binders

We will be going through all the concepts and code snippets discussed in *Chapter 5*, *Executing Distinctive Approaches like GetX, GetIt, and Binder*. We are going to create the same screens we created in the previous chapter but with an updated technique. So, technically the output of every technique will be the same (a cart application where you can add/remove items from the cart) but with entirely different code running behind each technique.

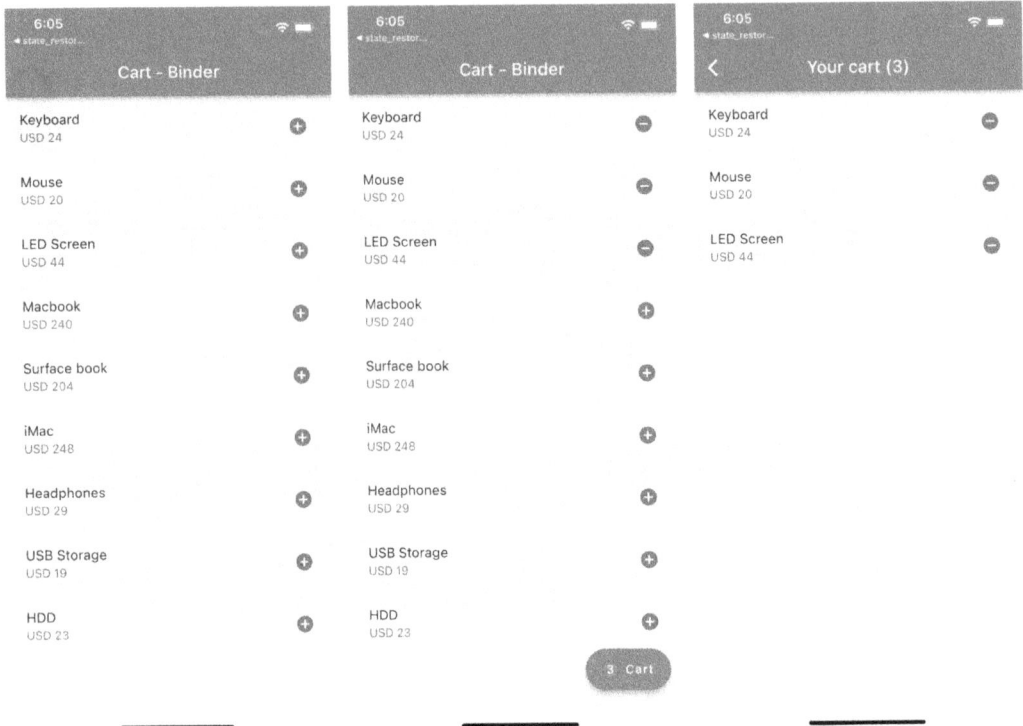

Figure 8.1 – Cart application screens

By the end of this chapter, you will be able to create Flutter apps from scratch using the three state-management techniques mentioned previously. You will also be provided with an optional challenge to get your brains working.

Technical requirements

To be able to fully understand and follow through this chapter, it is required that you have gone through *Chapter 5*, *Executing Distinctive Approaches like GetX, GetIt, and Binder*, thoroughly. This is because we will be putting all those concepts and code keywords directly to use in this chapter.

We will be using most of the code from the previous chapter, so it is also required that you have followed all the steps in *Chapter 7, Manipulating a Shopping Cart Application through BLoC, Provider, and React-Based Approaches.*

All the code in this chapter is uploaded (in complete form) here: `https://github.com/PacktPublishing/Managing-State-in-Flutter-Pragmatically/tree/main/ch8`.

> **Important Note**
> Since we are now creating intermediate-level working apps, it is expected that you will implicitly understand and execute certain basic steps, such as creating a new app, creating model classes, adding import statements, and so on.

Creating a cart app with GetX

We will be reusing the same screens we created in the previous chapters, with some editions specific to GetX. Let's begin by creating our cart application using GetX:

1. Create a new Flutter app named `cart_getx` and add dependencies for GetX from `pub.dev`.

2. Copy the `item.dart` file from the previous chapter's code into the `lib` folder of your `cart_getx` app. Make sure to add the dependency for the `equatable` package from `pub.dev`.

3. Create a new file named `cart_controller.dart` and add the following class:

```
class Cart {
  List<Item> items = populateItems();

  List<Item> cart = [];

  Cart({required this.cart});
}
```

This is a very simple, self-explanatory class that holds our static item list and an initially empty cart.

Don't forget to add the following import in order to make the `Item` class work:

```
import 'item.dart';
```

4. In the same `cart_controller.dart` file, underneath the `Cart` class, add the following controller class:

```
class CartController extends GetxController {
  var cart = (Cart(cart: [])).obs;

  void addItemToCart(Item item) {
    cart.value.cart.add(item);
    update();
  }

  removeItemFromCart(Item item) {
    cart.value.cart.remove(item);
    update();
  }
}
```

As we studied in *Chapter 5*, *Executing Distinctive Approaches like GetX, GetIt, and Binder*, this controller extends the functionality from the GetX package's `GetxController` class to make our cart class observable using a `.obs` keyword, along with being able to trigger an update to the UI using an `update` function.

Don't forget to add the import for the `get` package:

```
import 'package:get/get.dart';
```

5. Inside `main.dart`, replace `MaterialApp` with `GetMaterialApp` to be able to use all the functionality from the GetX package. Also, update the value of the `title` property of the `MyHomePage` constructor to `'Cart - GetX'`. Your `MyApp` class should now look something like this:

```
class MyApp extends StatelessWidget {
  @override
  Widget build(BuildContext context) {
    return GetMaterialApp(
      title: 'Flutter Demo',
      theme: ThemeData(
        primarySwatch: Colors.blue,
      ),
      home: MyHomePage(title: 'Cart - GetX'),
```

```
      );
    }
  }
```

Don't forget to import the dependency for the GetX package:

```
import 'package:get/get.dart';
```

6. Inside the _MyHomePageState class, remove everything and add the following code:

```
@override
Widget build(BuildContext context) {
  // One
  Get.put(CartController());
  // Two
  return GetBuilder(
    builder: (CartController controller) {
      return Scaffold(
        appBar: AppBar(
          title: Text(widget.title),
        ),
        body: ListView(
          // Three
          children: controller.cart.value.items
              .map(
                (e) => ListTile(
                  title: Text(e.name ?? ''),
                  subtitle: Text("USD " + (e.price ??
                  '')),
                  trailing: IconButton(
                    icon: Icon(
                      controller.cart.value.cart.
                      contains(e) ? Icons.remove_
                      circle : Icons.add_circle,
                    ),
                    onPressed: () {
                      // Four
```

```
                      if (!controller.cart.value.
                      cart.contains(e))
                        controller.addItemToCart(e);
                      else
                        controller.removeItemFromCart
                        (e);
                  },
                ),
              ),
            )
            .toList(),
        ),
        // Five
        floatingActionButton:
         controller.cart.value.cart.isEmpty
            ? null
            : FloatingActionButton.extended(
                onPressed: () {
                  Navigator.of(context).push(
                    MaterialPageRoute(
                      builder: (context) =>
                        CartPage(),
                    ),
                  );
                },
                label: Row(
                  children: [
                    Container(
                      padding: const
                      EdgeInsets.all(4),
                      decoration: BoxDecoration(
                        shape: BoxShape.circle,
                        color: Colors.red,
                      ),
```

```
                           // Six
                           child: Text(controller.cart.
                           value.cart.length.toString()),
                        ),
                        SizedBox(width: 8),
                        Text('Cart'),
                     ],
                  ),
               ),
            );
         },
      );
   }
```

Don't forget to add the import:

```
import 'cart_controller.dart';
```

You have now created the main screen of your application (see the leftmost screen in *Figure 8.1*). There are highlighted comments inside the preceding code, which are explained in order as follows:

- One: We put our `CartController` class inside of GetX's controller stack so that we can retrieve the same instance of the `CartController` class elsewhere.

- Two: We wrap our page with a `GetBuilder` widget to get the latest instance of our `CartController` class. We do that to update our page whenever an item is added/removed from the cart.

- Three: `ListView` gets populated with the static list of items from the `Cart` class, which we added in *step 3*.

- Four: If the cart already contains the item, the item gets removed from the cart, and vice versa, using the controller instance, which we are getting from the `builder` property in the `GetBuilder` widget.

- Five: The `FloatingActionButton` widget is visible only if the cart has any items in it.

- Six: The `FloatingActionButton` widget shows the count of the items in the cart.

7. Create a new file named cart_page.dart and add the following code:

```dart
import 'package:flutter/material.dart';
import 'package:get/get.dart';

import 'cart_controller.dart';

class CartPage extends StatefulWidget {
  CartPage();

  @override
  _CartPageState createState() => _CartPageState();
}

class _CartPageState extends State<CartPage> {
  @override
  Widget build(BuildContext context) {
    return GetBuilder(
      builder: (CartController controller) {
        return Scaffold(
          appBar: AppBar(
            title: Text("Your cart
            (${controller.cart.value.cart.length})"),
          ),
          body: ListView(
            children: controller.cart.value.cart
                .map(
                  (e) => ListTile(
                    title: Text(e.name ?? ''),
                    subtitle: Text("USD " + (e.price
                    ?? '')),
                    trailing: IconButton(
```

```
                icon: Icon(Icons.remove_circle),
                onPressed: () {
                    controller.removeItemFromCart
                    (e);
                },
              ),
            ),
          )
        .toList(),
      ),
    );
  }
);
}
}
```

This is almost the same as the `cart_page.dart` file from the sections in the previous chapter. The only change is the wrapping of the `GetBuilder` widget around `Scaffold` and the `onPressed` function of the `IconButton` widget.

There is only one more thing that needs to be done before you can run the app. Navigate to the `main.dart` file and add the missing import:

```
import 'cart_page.dart';
```

That's it! The app is done. Now, if you try to run the app, everything should work.

Optional challenge – GetX

Try adding a quantity to every item that is being added. You might need to change the UI and UX of the application as well to make it work. The updated quantity of every item should reflect inside the `cart_page.dart` file, as well as in the main list.

We are done with creating our cart application using GetX. In the next section, we will be creating our cart application using GetIt.

Creating a cart app with GetIt

Let's create our cart application using GetIt. You will need to create a new Flutter app named `cart_get_it`, add a dependency for `get_it` and `equatable` from `pub.dev`, and copy the `item.dart` file from the previous section's code into your `lib` folder. Let's get started:

1. Create a new file named `cart_model.dart` and add the following code:

```dart
import 'package:flutter/material.dart';

import 'item.dart';
import 'main.dart';

// One
class CartModel extends ChangeNotifier {

  // Two
  List<Item> items = populateItems();

  List<Item> cart = [];

  // Three
  void addItemToCart(Item item) {
    var newCart = <Item>[];
    newCart.addAll(cart);
    newCart.add(item);
    cart = newCart;
    notifyListeners();
  }

  removeItemFromCart(Item item) {
    var newCart = <Item>[];
    newCart.addAll(cart);
    newCart.remove(item);
    cart = newCart;
    notifyListeners();
  }
```

```
// Four
CartModel() {
  Future.delayed(Duration(milliseconds:
  100)).then((_) => getIt.signalReady(this));
  }
}
```

This is the `cart_model.dart` file that is responsible for updating your cart every time the user adds/removes an item. The code has highlighted comments, which are explained in order as follows:

- One: The GetIt package uses `ChangeNotifier` to listen to changes, so we won't be needing to add an import for `get_it` in this file.

- Two: The list of items is populated statically using the function inside `item.dart`.

- Three: The two functions are responsible for adding/removing items from the cart and then notifying the listeners to update the UI.

- Four: The `signalReady` function needs to be called with a delay to register it as a singleton (which is to be done in the step after next). If we don't call it with a delay, we will get a bad state exception, which will tell us that the instance of `CartModel` is not yet available in GetIt.

2. Add a global instance for GetIt inside the `main.dart` file, just above the main function:

```
GetIt getIt = GetIt.instance;
```

You will have to add the import for `get_it`:

```
import 'package:get_it/get_it.dart';
```

3. Inside the `main` function of `main.dart` file, you will have to register our `CartModel` class as a singleton with `signalsReady` property set to `true` so that the code added in the previous step knows it's inside GetIt and is available to be used. Your `main` function should look something like this now:

```
void main() {
  getIt.registerSingleton<CartModel>(CartModel(),
  signalsReady: true);
```

```
  runApp(MyApp());
}
```

Don't forget to add the import for the `CartModel` class:

```
import 'cart_model.dart';
```

4. Update your `title` property to reflect the new name that appears on your home
    page to `'Cart - GetIt'`:

```
class MyApp extends StatelessWidget {
  @override
  Widget build(BuildContext context) {
    return MaterialApp(
      title: 'Flutter Demo',
      theme: ThemeData(
        primarySwatch: Colors.blue,
      ),
      home: MyHomePage(title: 'Cart - GetIt'), //
      Updated code
    );
  }
}
```

5. Remove everything inside the `_MyHomePageState` class in the `main.dart` file
    and add the following `initState` function:

```
@override
void initState() {
  getIt.isReady<CartModel>().then((_) =>
  getIt<CartModel>().addListener(update));
  // Alternative
  // getIt.getAsync<CounterModel>().
    addListener(update);

  super.initState();
}
```

As soon as the page loads, it is going to check whether our CartModel instance is ready. If it is, it will add a function named update to it as a listener. This means every time our CartModel instance gets updated, this update function will be triggered. Since update is not created, this code is going to give errors. Let's create this function in the next step.

Alternatively, you can also use the getAsync method to carry out the same functionality.

6. Add the update function just after the initState function:

```
void update() => setState(() => {});
```

This is a simple setState function that will be called every time our CartModel instance gets updated. You could also put this setState function directly as an argument in the previous step. We created a separate function for simplicity and readability.

7. Add the following code after the update function:

```
@override
Widget build(BuildContext context) {
  // One
  var model = getIt<CartModel>();
  var cart = model.cart;

  // Two
  return FutureBuilder(
    future: getIt.allReady(),
    builder: (context, snapshot) {
      if (snapshot.hasData)
        return Scaffold(
          appBar: AppBar(
            title: Text(widget.title),
          ),

          // Three
          body: ListView(
```

```
children: getIt<CartModel>()
  .items
  .map(
    (e) => ListTile(
      title: Text(e.name ?? ''),
      subtitle: Text("USD " + (e.price
        ?? '')),
      trailing: IconButton(
        icon: Icon(
          cart.contains(e) ? Icons.
          remove_circle :
          Icons.add_circle,
        ),
        onPressed: () {

          // Four
          if (!cart.contains(e))
            model.addItemToCart(e);
          else
            model.removeItemFromCart(e);
        },
      ),
    ),
  )
  .toList(),
),
floatingActionButton: cart.isEmpty
  ? null
  : FloatingActionButton.extended(
      onPressed: () {
        Navigator.of(context).push(
          MaterialPageRoute(
            builder: (context) =>
            CartPage(),
          ),
        );
```

```
                    },
                  label: Row(
                    children: [
                      Container(
                        padding: const
                        EdgeInsets.all(4),
                        decoration: BoxDecoration(
                          shape: BoxShape.circle,
                          color: Colors.red,
                        ),
                        child: Text(
                        cart.length.toString()),
                      ),
                      SizedBox(width: 8),
                      Text('Cart'),
                    ],
                  ),
                ),
              );

    // Five
    return Column(
      mainAxisAlignment: MainAxisAlignment.center,
      mainAxisSize: MainAxisSize.min,
      children: [
        Text('Waiting for initialisation'),
        SizedBox(
          height: 16,
        ),
        CircularProgressIndicator(),
      ],
    );
    },
  );
}
```

You are done creating your main screen containing the items list (see the left-hand screen in *Figure 8.1*). The preceding code has some highlighted comments, which are explained in order as follows:

- One: We retrieve the latest updated instance of our CartModel instance from the global getIt variable declared in step 2.

- Two: The FutureBuilder widget here helps us build the UI using the allReady function inside getIt. Since we have given a delay of 100 milliseconds, the UI will pick this up as a Future value.

- Three: The list of items will be populated using the static list declared inside CartModel.

- Four: We will directly call functions inside our CartModel instance to add/remove items from the cart.

- Five: Since we are using FutureBuilder with an if condition inside it, we will have to return something after our if condition. This UI will be displayed for 100 milliseconds at maximum since we have given the same amount of delay before signaling the instance as ready.

Don't forget to import the following for CartPage:

```
import 'cart_page.dart';
```

You will be getting an error here because this file doesn't exist yet. Let's create it.

8. Create a new file named cart_page.dart and add the following code:

```
import 'package:flutter/material.dart';

import 'cart_model.dart';
import 'main.dart';

class CartPage extends StatefulWidget {
  CartPage();

  @override
  _CartPageState createState() => _CartPageState();
}

class _CartPageState extends State<CartPage> {
```

```
// One
@override
void initState() {
  getIt.isReady<CartModel>().then((_) =>
  getIt<CartModel>().addListener(update));
  // Alternative
  // getIt.getAsync<CounterModel>().
     addListener(update);

  super.initState();
}

void update() => setState(() => {});

@override
Widget build(BuildContext context) {

  // Two
  var model = getIt<CartModel>();
  var cart = model.cart;
  return Scaffold(
    appBar: AppBar(
      title: Text("Your cart (${cart.length})"),
    ),
    body: ListView(
      children: cart
          .map(
            (e) => ListTile(
              title: Text(e.name ?? ''),
              subtitle: Text("USD " + (e.price ??
              '')),
              trailing: IconButton(
                icon: Icon(Icons.remove_circle),

                // Three
                onPressed: () {
```

```
                         model.removeItemFromCart(e);
                    },
                ),
            ),
          )
        .toList(),
      ),
    );
  }
}
```

We are done creating the cart page (see the center and right-hand screens in *Figure 8.1*), which is going to contain the items that have been added by the user from the first screen. The preceding code has some highlighted comments, which are explained in order as follows:

- One: This is the same as we did in *steps 5 and 6*. We are telling this page to call `setState` whenever the instance of our `CartModel` gets updated.

- Two: Retrieving the updated instance of `CartModel`.

- Three: Removing an item from the cart using the function inside `CartModel`.

And we are done with creating our cart application using GetIt.

In the next section, we will look into how to create a cart application using Binder. This will be our last technique in this chapter, as well as in this book. You can try the previous section's optional challenge using GetIt as well, and compare which one turns out better for you.

Creating a cart app using Binder

Let's create our cart application using Binder. You will need to create a new Flutter app named `cart_binder`, add a dependency for `binder` and `equitable` from `pub.dev`, and copy the `item.dart` file from the previous section's code into your `lib` folder. Let's get started:

1. Create a new file named `cart_model.dart` and add the following imports first:

    ```
    import 'package:binder/binder.dart';
    import 'item.dart';
    ```

2. Add the following line for getting the static list of items to be shown on the main screen:

```
List<Item> items = populateItems();
```

3. Add the `CartModel` class underneath the `items` variable declaration:

```
class CartModel {
  List<Item> cart;


  CartModel({required this.cart});
}
```

This class is simple responsible for holding our `cart` variable:

```
final cartRef = StateRef(CartModel(cart: []));


final cartViewLogicRef = LogicRef((scope) =>
CartViewLogic(scope));
```

As we studied in *Chapter 5, Executing Distinctive Approaches like GetX, GetIt, and Binder*, we create a reference variable to read the latest value of objects and a view logic reference to update the value from the UI; we are doing the same for our cart application. The `cartRef` variable holds our latest and updated cart, with an empty array being the initial value, and `cartViewLogicRef` updates the values in the `CartViewLogic` class. The `CartViewLogic` class doesn't exist yet, so let's create it.

4. Add the following class beneath the reference variables declaration:

```
class CartViewLogic with Logic {
  const CartViewLogic(this.scope);


  @override
  final Scope scope;


  void addToCart(Item item) {
    read(cartRef).cart.add(item);
    var updatedCart = CartModel(cart:
    read(cartRef).cart);
    write(cartRef, updatedCart);
```

```
    }

    void removeFromCart(Item item) {
      read(cartRef).cart.remove(item);
      var updatedCart = CartModel(cart:
      read(cartRef).cart);
      write(cartRef, updatedCart);
    }
  }
```

This uses the `Logic` class from the `Binder` package, which is responsible for keeping all the boilerplate code that allows us to reference our class from the UI through the `cartViewLogicRef` variable. This class holds the add and remove functions that update the latest values of the cart using the write function.

5. Inside the `main.dart` file, add the three imports first:

```
import 'package:binder/binder.dart';
import 'cart_model.dart';
import 'cart_page.dart';
```

6. Wrap your `MaterialApp` widget with a `BinderScope` widget to be able to use all the functionality encapsulated in the package. Your `MyApp` class should look something like this:

```
class MyApp extends StatelessWidget {
  const MyApp({Key? key}) : super(key: key);
  @override
  Widget build(BuildContext context) {
    return BinderScope(
      child: MaterialApp(
        title: 'Flutter Demo',
        theme: ThemeData(
          primarySwatch: Colors.blue,
        ),
        home: const MyHomePage(title: 'Cart -
        Binder'),
      ),
```

```
      );
    }
  }
```

We also updated our title relative to our section name.

7. Remove everything inside the _MyHomePageState class in the main.dart file and add the following code:

```
@override
Widget build(BuildContext context) {

  // One
  final myCartRef = context.watch(cartRef);
  return Scaffold(
    appBar: AppBar(
      title: Text(widget.title),
    ),
    body: ListView(

      // Two
      children: items
          .map(
            (e) => ListTile(
              title: Text(e.name ?? ''),
              subtitle: Text("USD " + (e.price ??
              '')),
              trailing: IconButton(
                icon: Icon(
                  myCartRef.cart.contains(e) ?
                  Icons.remove_circle :
                  Icons.add_circle,
                ),
                onPressed: () {

                  // Three
                  if (!myCartRef.cart.contains(e)) {
```

```
                    context.use(cartViewLogicRef
                    ).addToCart(e);
                } else {
                    context.use(cartViewLogicRef
                    ).removeFromCart(e);
                }
            },
        ),
    ),
)
    .toList(),
),

// Four
floatingActionButton: myCartRef.cart.isEmpty
    ? null
    : FloatingActionButton.extended(
        onPressed: () {
            Navigator.of(context).push(
                MaterialPageRoute(
                    builder: (context) => CartPage(),
                ),
            );
        },
        label: Row(
            children: [
                Container(
                    padding: const EdgeInsets.all(4),
                    decoration: const BoxDecoration(
                        shape: BoxShape.circle,
                        color: Colors.red,
                    ),
                    child: Text(myCartRef.cart.
                    length.toString()),
                ),
                const SizedBox(width: 8),
```

```
                    const Text('Cart'),
           ],
        ),
      ),
    );
}
```

We are done with our main screen containing the list of items that can be added to the cart (see the left-hand screen in *Figure 8.1*). The preceding code has some highlighted comments, which are explained in order as follows.

- One: Retrieving the latest reference of our cart using the `watch` function from Binder.

- Two: The items are directly populated using the globally declared `items` variable in `cart_model.dart`.

- Three: The use function from the Binder package allows us to call functions inside our `CartViewLogic` class.

- Four: The `cart` variable from the `CartViewLogic` class is used to display `FloatingActionButton` and the number of items inside the cart. The `CartPage` navigation is going to give an error right now because this doesn't exist yet. Let's create it.

8. Create a new file named `cart_page.dart` and add the following code:

```
import 'package:cart_binder/cart_model.dart';
import 'package:flutter/material.dart';
import 'package:binder/binder.dart';

class CartPage extends StatefulWidget {
  const CartPage({Key? key}) : super(key: key);

  @override
  _CartPageState createState() => _CartPageState();
}


class _CartPageState extends State<CartPage> {
  @override
  Widget build(BuildContext context) {
```

```
// One
final cart = context.watch(cartRef).cart;
return Scaffold(
  appBar: AppBar(
    title: Text("Your cart (${cart.length})"),
  ),
  body: ListView(
    children: cart
        .map(
          (e) => ListTile(
        title: Text(e.name ?? ''),
        subtitle: Text("USD " + (e.price ?? '')),
        trailing: IconButton(
          icon: const Icon(Icons.remove_circle),

          // Two
          onPressed: () {
            context.use(cartViewLogicRef
            ).removeFromCart(e);
          },
        ),
      ),
    )
        .toList(),
  ),
);
}
}
```

We have created our cart screen (see the center and right-hand screens in *Figure 8.1*). The highlighted comments in the preceding code are explained in order as follows:

- One: Retrieving the latest updated instance of the cart from the `cartRef` variable using the `watch` function from Binder

- Two: Removing the current item from the cart using the `use` function from Binder

And here we are, our cart application completed using Binder. Go ahead and run the application now.

Summary

This marks the end of our cart application building using all the techniques discussed in the book. In this chapter, specifically, we used observables in GetX to make our class objects automatically update, we used GetIt to update our app's state without using `BuildContext`, and we took a thorough look into how to bind the UI with reference variables and a view logic class using Binder to update the app's state.

You should now be able to create Flutter apps using the different state management techniques discussed in this chapter and the previous ones. You should be able to differentiate between ways to manage the application's state using different techniques. You might not be able to remember everything about the techniques, but that's nothing to worry about; you don't need to memorize everything. Practice will clear the fog!

In the next and final chapter of the book, we will discuss some potential ways to decide which technique you should use for certain sorts of applications in Flutter. We will be doing that by quickly summarizing the specifics of every technique and analyzing the features and advantages that each technique offers, and trying to fit that into different sorts of applications. That way, we will be able to know which sort of applications can be built using which techniques. The goal is to teach you to pick a technique whenever you have an app idea in your mind.

9
Comparative State Management Analysis: When to Use What?

Finally, we are done with studying and implementing most of the state management techniques used in the Flutter world. Since technology is ever-growing, you might find some techniques that aren't discussed in the book or some that may not exist at all while this book is being written and emerge afterward, but you do not need to worry about those. As long as you know the basic idea and the reason for learning about state management, you can always learn any new technique that comes up any time in the future.

With that being said, let's move on to our final chapter of the book, where we will hover over and revisit all the techniques we discussed in this book for a refresher, and then learn to decide where to use which technique. This chapter is divided into five major sections, as outlined here:

- **Revisiting the techniques**—We will briefly go through all the different techniques we have discussed and revise some important concepts and keywords discussed in each of them.

- **Mapping different techniques to different application ideas**—A comparative analysis: we will see different application ideas and try to map them to different state management techniques. This is the section where we will learn to decide which technique is suitable for which sort of application.

- A brief discussion on good architecture

- Author's choice of state management technique—Hybrid approach

- A short overview of statement management decision-making

Technical requirements

To be able to fully understand and follow through this chapter, it is required that you go through all the previous chapters beforehand, especially the code parts. This is because we will be revising all of the techniques in a high-level fashion (such as omitting the boilerplate code setups in most of the techniques and jumping directly to the **user interface** (**UI**) code for a quick refresher).

There is no code repository for this chapter, as this chapter is just to help you decide which technique would suit you best in certain circumstances.

Revisiting the techniques

Let's begin by revising the concepts and keywords of all the techniques we have learned in this book, starting from the very basic—that is, `setState`.

> Note
>
> Some techniques (such as `InheritedWidget` and `InheritedModel`, **Business Logic Component** (**BLoC**), *Cubit*, and so on) have been coupled together in a single subsection due to major similarities.

setState

We studied that setState is the simplest form of state management in Flutter. This technique is used to rebuild your current widget and the widgets inside it whenever there is user interaction inside your widget. Some key points that we studied for setState include the following:

- It is a function that allows you to rebuild your widget's build method with updated variables' values. Here is a short reminder of how it is used in the counterexample application:

```
void _incrementCounter() {
    setState(() {
        _counter++;
    });
}
```

- Passing the data to other screens is done through constructor variables, whereby the next screen's constructor accepts a parameter that is passed from the first page. Here is an example of their usage:

```
Navigator.of(context).push(
        MaterialPageRoute(
            builder: (context) => PageTwo(counter:
            _counter),
        ),
    );
```

The PageTwo class looks something like this, with the counter parameter inside its constructor:

```
class PageTwo extends StatefulWidget {
    int counter;

    PageTwo({required this.counter});

    @override
    _PageTwoState createState() => _PageTwoState();
}
```

- Data is returned to the first screen in two different ways, outlined as follows:

  - The first way is by using the pop function from the second screen and receiving it in the first screen, as illustrated here:

    ```
    Navigator.of(context).pop(widget.counter);
    ```

    Here is the first screen receiving end:

    ```
    var value = await Navigator.of(context).push(
        MaterialPageRoute(
          builder: (context) => PageTwo(counter:
          _counter),
        ),
      );
    ```

  - The second way is by using callbacks (passing functions in constructors). Here is some example code for the first screen:

    ```
    Navigator.of(context).push(
        MaterialPageRoute(
          builder: (context) => PageTwo(
            counter: _counter,
            callback: (value) {
              setState(() {
                _counter = value;
              });
            },
          ),
        ),
      );
    ```

    The PageTwo class looks something like this, with the counter and callback parameters inside its constructor:

    ```
    class PageTwo extends StatefulWidget {
      final Function(int) callback;
      int counter;

      PageTwo({required this.counter, required
      this.callback});
    ```

```
    @override
    _PageTwoState createState() => _PageTwoState();
}
```

Here, we are calling the callback function inside the `PageTwo` class's `_incrementCounter` function:

```
void _incrementCounter() {
    setState(() {
        widget.counter++;
    });
    widget.callback(widget.counter); // new code
}
```

InheritedWidget and InheritedModel

`InheritedWidget` and `InheritedModel` are more or less the same except for a minor difference in the `aspect` values. We have some boilerplate code that is to be written before we actually manage our state. You can revisit the boilerplate code in *Chapter 2, The Core Building Blocks of State Management*. We will be revisiting the usage part of that boilerplate code here. Some key points from `InheritedWidget` are noted here:

- The `InheritedWidget` root sits at the top of the widget tree and wraps the whole application in order to inject the state down to every widget, as illustrated in the following code snippet:

```
MyInheritedWidget(
    child: MyHomePage(title: 'Flutter Demo Home Page'),
    counter: 1,
),
```

The `InheritedWidget` root also takes the initial value of whichever object type you are using in your application. In this case, it was an integer type with an initial value of 1.

- The `.of` method is used to access the latest value of the variable from the widget tree, as follows:

```
Text(MyCounterInheritedWidget.of(context).counterValue.
toString())
```

- Similarly, the functions can be accessed in the same way, as illustrated here:

```
MyCounterInheritedWidget.of(context).incrementCounter();
```

`InheritedModel` is similar to `InheritedWidget` but with some optimization in the boilerplate code. Here, you can choose if you want to rebuild a certain widget or not by using `aspect`. The `aspect` value is passed inside the `inheritFrom` method, as illustrated in the following code snippet:

```
InheritedModel.inheritFrom<MyInheritedWidget>(context, aspect:
1)!
        .data
        .counterValue
        .toString()
```

The `aspect` value on which the widget needs to be rebuilt is defined in the boilerplate code, and that specific value is passed in the preceding code when you want to code to rebuild this specific widget.

Provider

Provider is simply all the boilerplate code inside `InheritedWidget` covered up in a single package. Some key takeaways from Provider are listed here:

- Provider is enabled by adding the dependency for the `Provider` package from `pub.dev`.
- Just as with `InheritedWidget`, Provider is wrapped around your application using the `ChangeNotifierProvider` widget in order to inject the state throughout the application.
- Provider is itself a wrapper around `InheritedWidget` that gets rid of all the boilerplate code that we wrote while setting up `InheritedWidget` and `InheritedModel`.
- Just as with `aspect` values, Provider has a property called `listen` that can be set to `false` when you don't want the widget to rebuild whenever an interaction has taken place.
- You can use `Provider.of<YourClass>(context)` to access the state.
- `Provider.of<YourClass>(context).yourVariable` is similar to `context.watch<YourClass>().yourVariable`.

Riverpod

Riverpod is an enhancement to Provider in terms of compile safety and null reading exceptions when using `read` or `watch` functions:

- The application is wrapped in a `ProviderScope` widget instead of a `ChangeNotifierProvider` widget.

- The `Consumer` widget is used to read state values, as illustrated in the following code snippet:

```
Consumer(
        builder: (context, watch, _) {
          final state = watch(counterProvider) as
          CounterModel;
          return Text('${state.count}');
        },
    )
```

- `StateNotifier` and `StateNotifierProvider` are used to set up your model class, which keeps your state. Their usage is illustrated in the following code snippet:

```
final counterProvider = StateNotifierProvider((ref) =>
CounterNotifier());

class CounterNotifier extends StateNotifier<CounterModel>
{
  CounterNotifier() : super(CounterModel(count: 0));
... ... ...
```

BLoC and Cubit

BLoC and *Cubit* are very similar to each other. We have similar keywords and ways to use both techniques in our application. Let's revisit what BLoC tells us, as follows:

- It enables us to decouple our business logic from our UI.

- It works on streams.

- We have `Event` classes, `State` classes, and `Bloc` classes, which enables us to set up the architecture of using a BLoC state management technique. Here is an example usage of BLoC architecture with the `BlocBuilder` widget:

```
BlocBuilder(
         bloc: BlocProvider.of<CounterBloc>(
         context),
         builder: (context, snapshot) {
           return Text(
             '${(snapshot as
             CounterState).count}',
             style: Theme.of(context)
             .textTheme.headline4,
           );
         },
       )
```

- Here is an example of calling an event in BLoC:

```
BlocProvider.of<CounterBloc>(context).
add(IncrementCounterEvent());
```

- We also studied a package called `Equatable` that allows us to compare object classes as a whole.

- We have `yield` keywords in order to tell the UI that something has been updated.

In Cubit, we came to know that we do not need `Event` classes and we can directly call functions from our UI inside our `Cubit` instance, just like this:

```
BlocProvider.of<CounterCubit>(context).increment();
```

We have an `emit` function instead of `yield` in Cubit, which updates our UI.

Redux

Redux is a unidirectional state management technique that is adopted from the React framework. It uses the `reducer` function to dispatch the UI changes and uses a `Store` class that is defined globally and that can be used at all places inside the application. Here are some revision points from what we studied about Redux:

- The application is wrapped with a `StoreProvider` widget, as illustrated in the following code snippet:

```
void main() {
  runApp(
    StoreProvider<CounterState>(
      store: store,
      child: MyApp(),
    ),
  );
}
```

  `store` is a global variable declared like this:

```
final store = Store<CounterState>(counterReducer,
initialState: CounterState());
```

- The `StoreConnector` widget is used to read the values of the variables from the state using the `converter` property, as illustrated in the following code snippet:

```
StoreConnector<CounterState, String>(
  converter: (store) => store.state.count.toString(),
  builder: (context, count) {
    return Text(
      count,
      style: Theme.of(context).textTheme.headline4,
    );
  },
),
```

- Functions are called using the `dispatch` function and by passing `Action` inside it as a parameter, as illustrated in the following code snippet:

```
onPressed: () => store.dispatch(Actions.Increment)
```

MobX

MobX is another sort of reactive state management technique that allows you to connect your data with your UI using observables. This package uses the least amount of boilerplate code to manage states. It always uses the `build_runner` package to generate most of the boilerplate code. Some key points for a MobX state management technique are compiled for you here:

- You need to create your model class with a `part` declaration on top of your file, like this:

```
part 'counter.g.dart';
```

You also need some keywords inside your class for the package to understand that this is to be autogenerated, as illustrated in the following code snippet:

```
class Counter = _Counter with _$Counter;

abstract class _Counter with Store {
  @observable
  int value = 0;

  @action
  void increment() {
    value++;
  }
}
```

- Now, you just need to run the following command and let the package do the magic:

```
flutter packages pub run build_runner build
```

- You use your `counter` variable value in your code in the simplest possible way using the `Observer` widget, like this:

```
Observer(
  builder: (_) => Text(
    '${counter.value}',
    style: const TextStyle(fontSize: 40),
  ),
),
```

GetX

GetX is one of the packages that are not only restricted to state management—you can also manage navigations inside your application using GetX efficiently. Some key takeaways from GetX are noted here:

- Your model class extends `GetxController` in order to be able to use GetX functionality from the package, as illustrated in the following code snippet:

```
class CounterController extends GetxController {
  var counter = (Counter(count: 0)).obs;

  void increment() {
    counter.value.count++;
    update();
  }
}
```

The `update` function comes from the `GetxController` class.

- In your UI, you use the `GetBuilder` function to get the latest value of your variables, as illustrated in the following code snippet:

```
GetBuilder(
            builder: (CounterController controller) {
              return Text(
                controller.counter.value
                .count.toString(),
                style: Theme.of(context)
                .textTheme.headline4,
              );
            },
          )
```

- You can also navigate to any new page using just a single line, as follows:

```
Get.to(MyNewPage());
```

GetIt

GetIt uses `setState` to update the UI and utilizes the power of **dependency injection** (**DI**) to make the state available throughout the application. There is no `BuildContext` parameter required to update and manage states anywhere in the application. Here is a brief overview of GetIt:

- A global instance is created that is used all over the application, as illustrated here:

  ```
  GetIt = GetIt.instance;
  ```

- The model class is registered as a singleton using the following code:

  ```
  getIt.registerSingleton<CounterModel>(CounterModel(),
  signalsReady: true);
  ```

- A global variable is then used to get the latest values of the state, like this:

  ```
  getIt<CounterModel>().counter.toString
  ```

- Similarly, the functions are also called using the global variable, as follows:

  ```
  getIt<CounterModel>().incrementCounter
  ```

Binder

Binder uses scopes and references to manage states. It also uses a `Logic` mixin from the Binder package to decouple the UI with business logic. Here is an overview of Binder:

- The `BinderScope` widget is wrapped around the `MaterialApp` widget in order to enable the functionality from the `Binder` package.

- After setting up the initial boilerplate code, you get the latest reference of your model class using the following code inside your `build` method:

  ```
  final counter = context.watch(counterRef);
  ```

  This is then used to get the latest value from the model, as follows:

  ```
  Text(counter.count.toString())
  ```

- The functions are called using the `use` function from the context, like this:

  ```
  context.use(counterViewLogicRef).increment()
  ```

Mapping different techniques to different application ideas

In this section, we will try to come up with application ideas and map them to the techniques we have studied in this book. We might not map every technique to the application ideas we discuss; rather, our primary goal is to understand how to look for a suitable state management solution when a certain application idea comes up in your mind or when you come across a situation whereby you have to decide on a state management technique for your next workplace project.

> **Important Note**
>
> Choosing a state management technique for applications is a subjective task, and you might find differences of opinions in this section with other books/articles/community personnel. At the end of the day, you can technically fit any state management technique to any application and it will work. It only comes down to how well managed your code is. Flutter has a very open architecture in this matter; you can literally create your own state management solution within your application by using a combination of multiple approaches as well. Your primary goal should be code understandability and maintainability.

setState

Let's first talk about `setState`. If you go out in the Flutter world and ask anyone about this, they would never recommend using `setState` in any application. That's true in almost every case because `setState` is ephemeral state management, which means it's made for local widget-specific state management and could get really messy when scaled up to different screens/widgets (a lot of callbacks and pulling data from the `pop` function—see *Chapter 6, Creating a Shopping Cart Application Using Basic Approaches*). However, you can use `setState` in simple portfolio applications that you might create for your own learning/experimenting purposes, just to learn about a need for the invention of state management solutions.

InheritedWidget/InheritedModel

You might want to skip `InheritedWidget` and `InheritedModels` while thinking of building an application because almost every other package uses these two techniques underneath—Provider, for example. Also, advanced state management packages have abstracted out all the boilerplate code that you need to write when developing applications through `InheritedWidget` and `InheritedModel`.

Provider/Riverpod

Provider and Riverpod can be used for almost any sort of application that is not so complex, having a decent backend that returns data in the form of **JavaScript Object Notation** (**JSON**) responses. Applications related to banks, productivity, tasks, to-do applications, and so on can be built using Provider and Riverpod. Since Provider is not reactive, it sometimes gets difficult to manage when your application starts to get bigger in terms of the code base.

JSON

If this term is new for you, check out this link for a brief understanding: `https://www.w3schools.com/whatis/whatis_json.asp`.

BLoC/Cubit

BLoC/Cubit is the go-to state management technique according to most people. It is fast, testable, and decouples the UI completely. Since it uses streams, it is good for building games as well. It can also be used in chat applications since there is a lot of user interaction within the application's state that needs to be reflected in the least possible time. BLoC can also be used in ride-hailing applications as well, along with entertainment applications such as Netflix, YouTube, and so on.

Distinctive approaches

Distinctive approaches such as GetX, GetIt, and Binder are usually used in specific cases where you want to have ease of use and spend less time building the architecture of the application. Scaling applications or adding/removing features from your application using these techniques might not be very feasible.

Note

Building an application architecture is a sort of a trade-off. You either spend more time building the architecture of the application using BLoC/Cubit/ Redux and make the management/refactoring/adding/removing of features easy, or you spend less time on the architecture setup and spend more time maintaining and adding features.

Redux

If you are building an application where you have a single source of data for the state in your application, *Redux* can be a good choice since it's unidirectional and it keeps its state all at a single place, as it is usually done in the React framework. Chat applications can be built using Redux as well, apart from BLoC.

MobX

If you have a lot of JSON data coming in and going out of your application through **application programming interfaces** (**APIs**), you can use *MobX* for code autogeneration. This will surely help you create functions automatically for converting the JSON data to Dart classes and vice versa (through the `build_runner` package).

> **Note**
>
> If *API* is a new term for you, check out this link for a quick brief: `https://www.mulesoft.com/resources/api/what-is-an-api`.

Creating a good architecture

Creating a good architecture is as important as choosing the right state management technique. Even the best state management techniques can be a pain if the architecture isn't laid down correctly.

There are some great architecture patterns out there for mobile applications, such as **Model-View-Controller** (**MVC**), **Model-View-Presenter** (**MVP**), **Model-View-ViewModel** (**MVVM**), and so on. You can read about them on the internet. However, this small section is added so that you know the basic idea behind good architecture.

First and foremost, your architecture should be about decoupling. Your UI classes should be totally independent of your model and domain classes, and the UI classes should only interact with the model classes through state management classes or controller classes. This is what a basic MVC implementation is: it separates your logic from your UI, which is the first step in making your project life easier. You should ideally start with MVC and upgrade according to your needs and goals.

You should also try to implement **SOLID** principles. SOLID is an acronym for five design principles intended to make software designs more understandable, flexible, and maintainable (`https://en.wikipedia.org/wiki/SOLID`). It stands for these five terms:

- **Single-responsibility principle**
- **Open-closed principle**
- **Liskov substitution principle**
- **Interface segregation principle**
- **Dependency inversion principle**

You can read about all of these in the link given previously.

You might not find all of these principles applied everywhere—I don't use all of them either—but ideally, the goal is to refactor our project to be the best in whatever way we can.

Author's choice of state management technique – a hybrid approach

In my recent few open source projects, I used an approach that I thought would work better for me. It might not be the best approach but it fits well with my use case, so I am going to share it with you in case you might think of testing this approach as well.

I once tried a mixture of `setState`, *Provider,* and *Cubit* for a simple application that used APIs to bring data in the form of JSON responses. That was just an experiment, but it turned out better than expected.

I used `setState` within the custom widgets I created for reusability—widgets such as custom standalone switches, and loaders. This made me independent of thinking about how to update specific widgets' states. It was simple—just update those widgets within themselves, irrespective of what is going on in the entire application.

I decided to use Cubit for state management in this project, probably because I had already tried Provider and `InheritedWidget` in my previous projects. I could have gone with BLoC, but since my application was not very huge, I thought I could use Cubit as it is slightly simpler than BLoC.

I used Provider to update the theme of my application. Using Provider only for the theme made something click in my mind because I once read an article in my Flutter-learning times that showed how to do this in the simplest possible and independent way using Provider. So, now, my application uses `ChangeNotifier` to notify of theme changes, and it sits on the topmost level of my application, even above the blocs (actually, there are no blocs on the top-level hierarchy; those would just be `BlocProviders` that register your blocs). The `main` function of my application looks something like this:

```
void main() async {
  WidgetsFlutterBinding.ensureInitialized();
  SharedPreferences prefs = await
  SharedPreferences.getInstance();
  var isDarkTheme = prefs.getBool(
  SharedPreferencesKeys.isDarkTheme);
  ThemeData theme;
  if (isDarkTheme != null) {
    theme = isDarkTheme ? darkTheme : lightTheme;
  } else {
    theme = lightTheme;
  }
  runApp(
    ChangeNotifierProvider<ThemeNotifier>(
      create: (_) => ThemeNotifier(theme),
      child: MyApp(),
      builder: (context, widget) => MyApp(),
    ),
  );
}
```

The code above the `runApp` function is responsible for checking if there is a user-preferred theme and applies whatever preferences (dark/light) are already set in the `SharedPreferences` plugin. If there is no preferred theme already set, the default `lightTheme` is applied. The `runApp` function wraps `ChangeNotifierProvider` with the type of the `ThemeNotifier` class (which is a simple class extending `ChangeNotifier`, similar to what we studied in *Chapter 3, Diving into Advanced State Management Approaches*), which has `setTheme` and `getTheme` functions.

The `MyApp` class looks something like this:

```
class MyApp extends StatelessWidget {
  @override
  Widget build(BuildContext context) {
    final themeNotifier = Provider.of
    <ThemeNotifier>(context);
    return MaterialApp(
      debugShowCheckedModeBanner: false,
      title: 'Novel Covid-19 Tracker',
      theme: themeNotifier.getTheme(),
      home: MultiBlocProvider(
        providers: [
          BlocProvider<GlobalInfoCubit>(
            create: (context) => GlobalInfoCubit()
            ..fetchGlobalStats(),
          ),
        ],
        child: HomePageMaster(),
      ),
    );
  }
}
```

Since the theme was already injected previously, we just need to get it using `Provider.of<ThemeNotifier>(context)`. The `BlocProvider` instances are instantiated here, independent of what's going on above the hierarchy.

The code shown in the preceding snippet is part of an open source project that can be found at this link: `https://github.com/wal33d006/novel_covid_19`. This code is not refactored completely to use cubits, but refactoring is in progress. Currently, `global_info.dart` uses a Cubit to manage its state.

> **Note**
> This could actually be a very good example to look at in the current conditions. We have both `setState` and Cubit in place, so it could be a good comparison to look at!

A short overview of state management decision-making

To sum up the philosophy of deciding when to choose what, we can look at the following statements:

- You might not use basic approaches such as `setState` and `InheritedWidget` in a lot of applications, but you can use them in your early stages where you practice small personal projects that have fewer screens and less user interaction.

- Productivity applications such as notes and to-do applications, financial applications, and applications that are straight in terms of interactions (getting data from a backend and displaying it; similarly, posting data based on user interaction) can be built using Provider or Riverpod.

- Redux can be used where you have a single source of state and you keep your application's state inside a single model/class. Redux can also be used for chat applications.

- BLoC is the go-to technique for almost any sort of application, ranging from entertainment, ride-hailing, and chat applications to email applications, and so on. Since BLoC uses streams, it might be a good choice for games as well.

- If you have a lot of JSON data coming in through any specific backend service, you can autogenerate it through the `build_runner` command and manage your state through MobX.

- You can also use a hybrid approach to architect your application. A combination of multiple state management techniques used carefully and wisely can be a blessing in disguise! But if you jumble up a lot of techniques together in a single application, you can mess it up and create an even bigger problem for yourself, so it's best to use a hybrid approach carefully.

> **Author's recommendation**
>
> If you decide to use a hybrid approach, you should keep one technique as your main state management technique and use any other to cover up for independent tasks, just as we had Provider for updating the theme throughout the application, which didn't affect any other part of the application at all and can be independently changed/updated to use some other technique at any future point in time.

The decision of choosing the correct state management technique is majorly dependent on the sort of application that you are going to build and the maximum complexity level that your application can reach up to. The business use case and the type of application should derive the appropriate state management technique.

Summary

We have studied and implemented a lot of state management techniques in this book. A lot of them might have appealed to you to a greater extent than others, while some of them might not have made it to your interest list. The whole idea of creating this book in the first place was not about making you the best decision-maker in terms of choosing a state management technique; rather, it was to make you understand the true power of every technique so that you know exactly when and where to use them. This whole book is a combination of different recipes that make you understand the pros and cons of every technique. If you have grasped the actual specifics of each technique, you will be able to instantly decide on a technique as soon as an application idea with details is put in front of you. After you are sufficiently well-versed in different techniques and you think you have improved in deciding on state management techniques, you can level yourself up in creating better architectures for your Flutter applications using the state management technique you just chose. This will enhance your architectural skills and you will learn to tackle problems that arise during the development phases (such as adding new features, testing applications, and so on). Correct state management techniques chosen as required by the application idea, along with good, stable architecture, could probably be the best thing that can happen to your Flutter application!

I, as the author of this book and a constant contributor to the developer community, would be immensely honored and delighted if this book helps you out in any way in your professional life. Best of luck and thank you for reading.

Happy choosing!

Packt>

Other Books You May Enjoy

If you enjoyed this book, you may be interested in these other books by Packt:

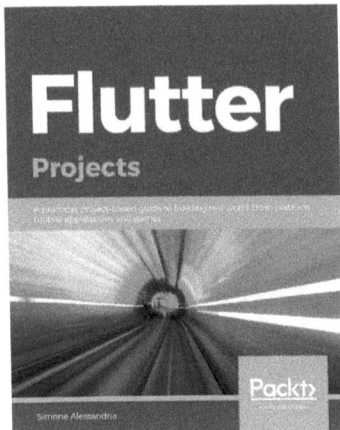

Flutter Projects

Simone Alessandria

ISBN: 978-1-83864-777-3

- Design reusable mobile architectures that can be applied to apps at any scale
- Get up to speed with error handling and debugging for mobile application development
- Apply the principle of 'composition over inheritance' to break down complex problems into many simple problems
- Update your code and see the results immediately using Flutter's hot reload

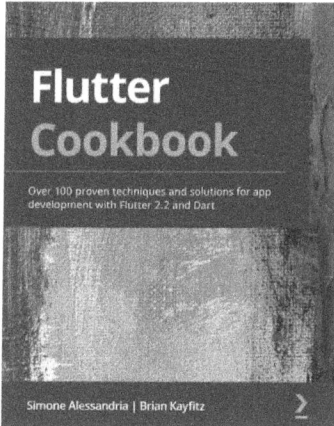

Flutter Cookbook

Simone Alessandria , Brian Kayfitz

ISBN: 978-1-83882-338-2

- Use Dart programming to customize your Flutter applications
- Discover how to develop and think like a Dart programmer
- Leverage Firebase Machine Learning capabilities to create intelligent apps
- Create reusable architecture that can be applied to any type of app
- Use web services and persist data locally
- Debug and solve problems before users can see them
- Use asynchronous programming with Future and Stream

Packt is searching for authors like you

If you're interested in becoming an author for Packt, please visit authors. packtpub.com and apply today. We have worked with thousands of developers and tech professionals, just like you, to help them share their insight with the global tech community. You can make a general application, apply for a specific hot topic that we are recruiting an author for, or submit your own idea.

Share Your Thoughts

Hi!

I am Waleed Arshad, author of Managing State in Flutter Pragmatically. I really hope you enjoyed reading this book and found it useful for increasing your productivity and efficiency in Flutter.

It would really help me (and other potential readers!) if you could leave a review on Amazon sharing your thoughts on book name here.

Your review will help me to understand what's worked well in this book, and what could be improved upon for future editions, so it really is appreciated.

Best Wishes,

Waleed Arshad

Index

S

T

Lightning Source UK Ltd.
Milton Keynes UK
UKHW031834060222
398281UK00004B/60

9 781801 070775